Small Space

Gloria Hall

ISBN 978-1-954345-25-6 (paperback)
ISBN 978-1-954345-26-3 (digital)

Copyright © 2021 by Gloria Hall

All rights reserved. No part of this publication may be reproduced, distributed, or transmitted in any form or by any means, including photocopying, recording, or other electronic or mechanical methods without the prior written permission of the publisher. For permission requests, solicit the publisher via the address below.

Rushmore Press LLC
1 800 460 9188
www.rushmorepress.com

Printed in the United States of America

For every woman who has suffered mental or physical abuse and is struggling to feel whole and free again—I pray that God will fill your heart with His love so that you will be able to completely forgive those who have mistreated you. I pray also that your spirits will be lifted, joy will replace the sadness in your heart, and you will be able to hold your head up and walk in freedom and assurance of God's grace.

Contents

Preface. vii
Introduction ix

1 My Last Night with Mama. 1
2 Weapons of Warfare 12
3 Oatmeal for Breakfast. 19
4 New Shoes 26
5 Sunday School 32
6 Two Weeks in Hell 35
7 Daddy's Talks 46
8 Three O'clock, School's Out 51
9 My Favorite Subjects 62
10 Raid Beets 70
11 Report Card Day 73
12 Summer at Aunt Tick's House 76
13 Stepping in the Mop Bucket. 81
14 Working at Leo's. 87
15 Boot Camp 105
16 Tour of Duty—Sunny California 111
17 A Bad Marriage 114
18 Is This the End? 123
19 I Want What She's Got. 142

About the Author 149

Preface

Too many adults today are harboring insecurities and hidden pains. They find it difficult trying to maneuver in a difficult world. My book addresses the abuse I endured at the hands of my stepmother. I lived a life full of fear, remorse, and suffering, tinged with self-blame.

I would like to use my experience to assure others who have been victims of mental or physical abuse that they can be free to live without further torment and shame. They are special, worthy, and loved by God; and only He can satisfy their spiritual hunger.

My book reveals how God guided and directed me to forgive by simply being obedient to Him and how He has aided me in understanding and realizing that He has a purpose and a plan for all of us.

Introduction

When I was five years old, my mother died, leaving my daddy to raise six small children alone. He soon remarried. My brothers and I endured physical and mental abuse at the hands of my stepmother who constantly told us that we were no good and would never amount to anything.

My two younger brothers and I lived in constant fear of the next beating, sometimes severe enough to keep us from school activities.

Although I excelled in spelling and public speaking, in general, school was difficult for me. My homelife kept me so mentally bound that I was unable to concentrate. I dreaded being beaten for bad report cards. For years, I had to deal with a low self-image.

Finally, upon running away from home, I joined the army and met and married my husband. The marriage was short-lived, and I was left to raise a young son on my own. I had no sense of security. As a consequence, I endured extreme loneliness and suffered severe financial and personal struggles.

I began praying and seeking God until one day, I realized He was my answer. He changed my whole outlook on life and made me feel I was worth something.

I discovered that God doesn't look down on us—we look down on ourselves.

1

My Last Night with Mama

Positioning my small frame comfortably on Mama's lap, I snuggled my head into the crook of her arm. It's nap time, and Mama and I were about to embark on our daily adventure. As we both turned the pages of the big "Mother Goose" nursery rhymes book, Mama read to me. But I couldn't fall asleep until she read my favorite rhyme, "Hickory Dickory Dock."

As the frisky little, brown mouse scampered up the side of the grandfather clock, I knew this one so well.

"Hickory dickory dock, the mouse ran up the clock," we read it together. "The clock struck one, the mouse ran down. Hickory-dickory dock."

The book was closed now. Mama couldn't read to me anymore. She was gone. I stood by the casket, barely able to see her, while Tommy, my oldest brother, was kneeling at a bench.

Why is he crying so? I wondered. *Mama is just sleeping, but I wish she would wake up. Is she taking a nap too?*

So much confusion and sadness surrounded the day; I didn't understand it all. I wished somebody would tell me what was wrong with Mama and why she wasn't coming home with us. At five years old, this was all very puzzling to me.

An aneurysm at the age of thirty-six had snatched Mama from us, leaving Daddy with six small children to raise alone. Daddy had often rushed her to the hospital because of the crippling headaches that occasionally gripped her and left her sick and weak.

One morning after suffering from one such horrific headache that had lasted through the night, Daddy carried Mama downstairs, gently placed her in the passenger side of the car, and hurriedly drove to the hospital. It wasn't long before he came home—this time, alone. Gathering us kids together, Daddy spoke in a soft, trembling voice that belied his grief:

"Mama's gone, boys."

No longer would Mama and I read nursery rhymes together. No longer would Mama hold me and rock me to sleep. No longer would I feel her warm, protective hand holding on to mine. No longer would I snuggle in her lap. No longer would I feel safe and secure. Mama's gone.

On the night of the funeral, I lay in bed, unable to sleep, staring into the darkness, thinking back over the day. All of a sudden, illuminated by the soft moonlight from the window across from my bed, Mama quietly and gently appeared in the closet entrance, beautifully dressed in purple, looking very much like she was on her way to church.

Surprised but delighted, I whispered, "Mama."

I sat up in bed to see her better and to be sure I wasn't dreaming. It was definitely my Mama. I wanted to run to her. I had so many unanswered questions. But fearing she might disappear, I didn't move. I just lay there, returning her gaze while we silently loved each other in the soft light.

Several seconds later, she was gone.

Even though my brothers were in bed at the time, I was sure they were asleep and hadn't seen her. I lay back down, feeling loved and closer to her than ever. I slept peacefully all night.

I told no one of the incident, but I could hardly wait until bedtime the next night. Finally in bed after an interminably long day, I lay again in the dark, hugging the covers up to my chin, peering over at the dark closet, anxiously waiting. My thoughts of the previous night were so vivid, I had every hope Mama would return.

If I don't breathe too hard, maybe she'll come, I thought. *If I'm real still and don't make any noise, she'll come.*

Before long, as I had hoped, Mama appeared. How I wanted to bury my face in that beautiful dress and feel her warm embrace. But I just lay still, watching her as I had the night before.

Night after night for two weeks, she came to me. She never spoke, but oh how I enjoyed our short, sweet visits. Then one night, as soon as she appeared in the doorway, my whole body stiffened in fear. When I could gather enough nerve, I quickly reached down and grabbed the covers from the foot of the bed and yanked them up over my head. Seconds later, I peeked, out and she was gone.

Chagrined, I lay there wondering what had happened. Not one of those nights had I been afraid. Not one of those nights had I questioned whether it was really her.

Why was I so afraid now? I mused. *Did I scare her away?*

Puzzled and confused, I finally drifted off to sleep with the covers still over my head.

I waited for her every night after that for months, but she never returned. Sometimes I woke up in the middle of the night thinking about her or hearing a sound that I thought was her. I craned my neck at the slightest noise I heard, hoping.

Now I wanted to see her just so I could tell her I wasn't afraid anymore. But would she ever come back?

How does a child grieve? I don't know. I don't remember grieving for Mama; unless intensely missing her could be interpreted as grieving. I don't even remember crying at the funeral.

For a very long time, I refused to believe that Mama had just died and left us. She wouldn't do that—not on purpose, anyway. I kept looking for her to walk in the front door or be downstairs when we got up in the morning. The closet she had appeared in didn't have a door on it, so sometimes I sat and stared into it, as if staring at it would bring her back. I felt as if some cruel joke had been played on us.

The street we lived on was quiet and serene, with trees standing like great giants in each yard, each tree quietly standing guard in front of the house it protected.

Most of the houses on our block were white, with the exception of Miss Flowers's house across the street. It stood out from all the others around it. Painted a bright yellow—her house was dotted with colorful, dainty flowers that adorned the front yard, the edge of the driveway, and the sidewalk. The lawn was always immaculate, nicely cut, and beautifully green. Even in the winter when the flowers died, I still thought her house was the prettiest.

Miss Flowers hung her clothes on the clothesline in her front yard, as did all the rest of the mothers. Nobody had clothes dryers. I suppose they had been invented, but they hadn't reached our neighborhood yet. Backyards were reserved for kids to play in.

We lived in one of the few two-story houses on the block. Our house was equipped with a kitchen, living room, and a utility room downstairs. I don't think they even make utility rooms anymore. The giant furnace that practically dominated the utility room, we kept cold and banked with ashes in the summer. In the wintertime, we shoveled it full of coal from the coal bin to heat the house. The heavy rumble of the pipes could be heard upstairs as the furnace did its work to heat up all the rooms.

Upstairs was the bathroom; right across the top of the stairs, Mama and Daddy's bedroom; and our bedroom where my brothers and I slept, me in the small bed and they in the larger two. Now that Mama was gone, our big, happy house seemed strangely quiet.

It must have been tough for Daddy to handle us and his own grief. He must have thought he couldn't care for us on his own or maybe he was afraid relatives would try and split us up. I do remember a relative there at the house after the funeral staring at me as if she wanted to snatch me. She never talked to me, but her eyes followed me everywhere I went. I tried not to get too close to her.

Daddy married again soon after Mama died. Our new stepmother, Joe, seemed to be on the defensive the day she moved into the house. She frowned most of the time and barked out orders rather than talking to us in civil tones. Already I didn't like her.

She rarely had a pleasant thing to say to anybody, and she certainly wasn't pretty like Mama. She was just the opposite from Daddy, who was a lot like the street we lived on—quiet and unassuming, soft-spoken, gentle, always the same. To me, they just didn't fit together.

She didn't allow any of us to talk about Mama. In fact, she tried to make us forget her altogether. Soon after she came, Daddy came home from work one day to find all of Mama's pictures cut up. I could hear them arguing in the living room. He was so mad at her.

He was able to salvage a few pictures she hadn't found, plus Mama's watch that Daddy gave me when I became a teenager. Even though my stepmother knew I had it, I kept it hidden so she wouldn't take it from me. It was my only link to Mama, aside from a photo of her that looks a lot like me.

Obviously to establish some disciplinary boundaries among us kids, Daddy eventually told her, "You take care of the little ones, and I'll take care of the big ones."

The "big ones" were my three older brothers. We "little ones" soon started getting yelled at on a regular basis. We learned quickly not to cross her. The more she yelled at us, the more I missed Mama.

Bedtime became my retreat time. I couldn't talk about Mama in the daytime or even call her name, but I could talk to her at night. I couldn't avoid my stepmother's wrath in the daytime, but at night in my bed, I felt safe. My thoughts and dreams were my own.

After Mama stopped coming to me at night, I missed her even more. Sometimes lying in bed, I could hear her softly reading to me.

"Let's turn the pages and read together, Mama," I'd say to the empty space. "Hickory dickory dock, the mouse ran up the clock. The clock struck one, the mouse ran down. Hickory dickory dock."

Then I'd bury my head in my pillow and cry myself to sleep.

My stepmother could cut up pictures, but she couldn't take away memories. I can still smell the wonderful homemade donuts Mama used to make for us. She covered the big wooden table in the kitchen from one end to the other with the floured cutout goodies, ready to fry soon as the grease was hot.

She was expert at mixing the dough, rolling it out just right with the rolling pin, cutting out the plump round shapes with the biscuit cutter, and dropping them one by one in hot oil. They smelled so good frying in the heavy black skillet. The aroma would waft past my nose through the house to the outside, making my mouth water. We could hardly wait for them to get done. Then when they cooled slightly, she dipped each one in cinnamon sugar or powdered sugar. It was impossible to choose which kind was best.

Mama sang or hummed while she cooked, and the kitchen was always a cozy and happy place to be. Even in the hot summertime, I liked being in the kitchen when Mama was cooking. I could feel her love even when she wasn't looking at me. How I missed that love. How I thrived on it. How I needed it now.

My stepmother's full name was Hazel Joseph, and everybody who knew her called her Joe. We called her Joe too.

She hadn't been with us very long when Daddy said to us little kids, "Hazel's been here long enough now. It's time you kids started calling her Mama instead of Joe. She feels bad that you're not already doing it. After all, she is your new mama."

My mouth felt dry and dirty every time I called her Mama. I felt like I was betraying my real mama. It was a very difficult thing to do, but we had to because she saw to it that we did. But when she began beating me, I rebelled and reverted back to calling her Joe. I felt like a yo-yo going back and forth.

"Don't be mad, Mama," I whispered. "I'm not doing this because I want to. You're my real mama, and she'll never make me forget you."

Within just a few weeks of her arrival, my stepmother began to slap me often. But I was determined not to be weak. I would have to learn to turn off my emotions and be tough. As time went on, loneliness was slowly being replaced by anger and, eventually, bitter hatred for her. Though I dared not let it show, I found myself wishing she would leave or die. I didn't care which.

Every time she and Daddy got into an argument, Donnie, Al, and I would exchange glances. And when we were sure she wasn't in earshot, one of us would whisper, "I hope she leaves."

The other two would chime in, "Yeah, us too."

And if the argument got really heated, our hopes would rise, especially when she yelled at Daddy, "I'm getting out of here. I don't have to stay here and take care of you and your kids. I can do better than this."

I never knew what the arguments were about. They argued so much, I never really listened. She packed her suitcase several times. We crossed our fingers, each time ever more hopeful. But she always later calmed down and unpacked. I don't think she had any real intentions of leaving. I just think she was trying to scare Daddy.

Tommy, Bob, and Richard were young teenagers when Mama died. I was too young to know how her death affected them since we weren't allowed to talk about her. But I imagined they talked among themselves and hurt as much as we did.

After graduating from high school, each one of them in turn left home to join various branches of the armed services.

Good for them, I used to think. *I'm sure they've had just about as much of Joe as they can take. I can't wait until I'm old enough to leave. I'm going to join the service too, just to get out of here.*

How I dreaded seeing each one of them go. But finally, there was just the three of us, me being the oldest; Donnie in the middle; and Al, the baby, who was only two at the time of Mama's death. Once they were all gone, she began treating us much worse than before. Where she had been slapping me before, now that my brothers were gone, the beatings started.

I missed my brothers terribly. My stepmother never told us when or if they wrote, though we were sure they must have. When one of them came home for a visit, we were overjoyed. But their visits were always too short, and there was very little communication among us when they were there. I'm sure it was because of the difference in our ages. And we were too afraid to tell them what was happening to us.

My stepmother began criticizing me for being no good and stupid.

"Your mama should have flushed you down the toilet when you was born because you're ugly and worthless," she said to me on several occasions. "Donnie should have been born a girl, and you should have been the boy because his legs are prettier than yours. Your legs are ugly, and you have butter heels. Why couldn't you have been the boy?"

I didn't know if I was supposed to answer that or not, so I thought it better that I didn't. I didn't know what *butter heels* were, but I knew it was something meant to be degrading. Nearly every day she found something else wrong with me. But even more humiliating was when she cursed at me and called me foul names, none of which I had heard before she came to live with us.

We learned to jump when she spoke. We also learned not to incur her wrath by talking without her permission or we ended up on the floor from a vicious backhand. "Speak when you're spoken to" became our silent theme.

A perfectionist when it came to house cleaning, she made sure every morning we cleaned the bathroom, made our beds, and dusted the living room before we left for school. We didn't mind cleaning, but we thought twice a day was too much, especially since hardly anybody ever came to visit.

In the afternoons, after school, we dusted the living room again, cleaned the bathroom again, and did whatever other chores were assigned to us. I'm sure we had the cleanest house in the neighborhood.

Wednesday was washing and ironing day. My job was to help get the wash started before I went to school. I kept an eye on the clock as I pulled all the bedclothes off all the beds to be washed. Joe always held up the sheets and examined them closely to see if one of us had wet the bed. It was easy to tell because a stain could easily be seen on a white sheet.

After my brothers all left, I began to occasionally wet the bed. I don't remember if Donnie or Al wet their bed or not. When I did, I was afraid to tell my stepmother and afraid not to tell her. I waited until washday, hoping she would let me load the washer myself or that she would put the sheets in without checking them, but she never did.

Dropping whatever she was doing, she took the sheets and held each one up to the light, studying it carefully as if hoping to detect a stain. If she did, she beat whoever wet the bed for wetting it and then for not telling her. I always tried to wake up in time to make it to the bathroom. Sometimes I made it; other times I didn't.

Each week before loading the sheets into the washer, she'd ask me, "Glo, did you wet the bed this week?"

If I hadn't, I didn't hesitate. "No, ma'am," I'd say, relieved that my sheets were clean.

If I had, I'd frantically search my mind for an answer I thought would keep me from getting a beating. I'd remember back to the morning after I'd wet and tried to clean up the wet spot with a wet cloth, hoping there would be no stain when it dried.

"One night this week, I started to wet the bed, but I woke up and made it to the bathroom," I said one day.

"No you didn't," she exclaimed almost gleefully, eyeing the stain on my sheets. "You did wet the bed, just like I thought. You could wake up if you wanted to. You're just lazy. You know you got to get punished. Go get me that switch."

Then I'd get a beating before going to school. Those came to be her favorite words, "Go get me that switch."

If washday was a day she had kept me home from school, after the washing was finished, I hung the clothes on the lines outside. As I hung the white sheets, my mind would travel back to when I was little and Mama had hung her clothes outside on this same line.

I remembered playing close by her side in my white, high-top baby shoes, gazing up at the fluffy clouds in the sky that resembled giant marshmallows—"pillows," I called them—as the snow-white sheets and pillowcases swayed back and forth in the gentle breeze discussing with the clouds the protocol for the day.

If I had gone to school on washday, I'd iron when I got home in the afternoon. I was good at ironing, and it was probably my favorite chore. My stepmother wanted everything ironed—from sheets and pillowcases to Daddy's shorts and work pants. There were times when there were so many clothes, it took me the entire evening to finish the ironing. I ironed up until dinnertime and then finished after we cleaned up the kitchen.

She usually ironed Daddy's white shirts for church. I was relieved whenever she did because it was a giant pain trying to get the wrinkles out of the cuffs and collars. But she left everything else for me. The ironing usually went smoothly because she starched Daddy's work shirts and most of our clothes. And when the starched clothes were sprinkled with water, this made ironing much easier.

Saturday was major cleaning day. I don't know what it was about Saturdays, but my stepmother acted as if Saturdays were cursed. She was always in a mood fouler than normal and yelled at us relentlessly, no matter how we scrubbed and polished. We tried to tiptoe noiselessly through the house as we did our chores.

We swept and mopped the kitchen and all the upstairs rooms. Beautiful, lush green plants sat regally all over the living room on tables, in front of the windows, and on the floor that she wouldn't let us touch. Because she cleaned each petal with olive oil, it took her over an hour to clean them all.

After mopping the living room floor, she'd get on her knees and take a portion of the mop in her hand to mop in the corners where some of the flowers sat. She did that portion of the cleaning because she didn't trust us around her plants and didn't want us breaking the leaves. I will say this for her. She definitely had a green thumb. Her plants rarely died. They were hearty and beautifully green in the summer and winter.

Although the floors were always clean, several times a day, she would take off her house slippers and tell one of us, "Go clean my shoes off." We took her shoes outside on the porch and scraped the bottoms together to clean off any dust or gravel that might have been on them. There rarely was.

I never knew what was wrong with her feet; but tough dark callous-like skin periodically formed on the sides and bottoms up to the point where she had to trim the toughest part off with a razor blade. She did this task while sitting in the kitchen where all the shavings fell on the floor. It was usually my job to get the broom and sweep them all up. She rarely did it herself.

We also had the menial task of keeping flies out of the house in the summertime. When a fly zoomed in an open door, she would yell, "Get that fly out of here!"

We knew the routine. Whoever wasn't busy had to walk around the house with a rolled-up newspaper looking for the fly. I felt ridiculous chasing after a fly, especially if someone happened to stop by.

For us, television was forbidden, and the living room was off-limits for sitting. We walked through it on our way upstairs or outside to the backyard. If Daddy was watching a program that looked interesting, we couldn't stop and watch it. The TV was never on in the daytime. He always turned it on when he came home from work.

And on the weekends, we were allowed to watch it at night only until bedtime, which was always at eight o'clock and only what they were watching. We didn't know what shows were good or bad, but if we had had a choice, we would have enjoyed watching cartoons on Saturday mornings.

Sitting against the wall in the living room next to the stairs was a small, red vinyl settee that squeaked loudly when anyone sat on it. Since we weren't allowed to sit in the chairs or on the couch, all three of us had to crowd on it when we did watch TV. There was really only room for two of us, not three.

Joe kept a close eye on us to see if one of us moved around. And if we did, she would look over at us and say, "Who's moving around on that settee?" so we had to keep very still. We felt like marble statues, unable to move or talk.

I sat on the couch once the whole time I lived at home, and that was when my Uncle Paul and Aunt Anne were visiting from Ohio.

Uncle Paul said to me at one point, "Come sit by me and tell me about yourself. How is school going?"

I shot a glance at my stepmother, but her face showed no reaction. I didn't want to get a beating after they went home for sitting on the couch.

In the wintertime, we were glad to retreat upstairs at eight o'clock for bed because it was dark and cold outside and we could lay in bed and talk quietly. But in the summertime, it was still hot and light out, and many of the neighborhood kids were still out playing. We wished we could be outside too. Trying to sleep in the summer heat was, at times, nearly impossible.

2

Weapons of Warfare

My stepmother's favorite form of punishment were switches—strong long, green ones that, in one swift blow, could wrap around your whole body. They made a swooshing sound as they sliced through the air to welt and cut through flesh. The force of the blows could take your breath away.

Sometimes I'd get beaten in the morning and could barely walk to school afterward. There were many times when she told me not to dress for gym because she had beaten me so badly that my legs and arms were bloody and had multiple welts and bruises. Before I'd leave for school, I'd go to the bathroom and try to wipe some of the blood off with a piece of toilet paper so it wouldn't stain my clothes, although sometimes it did.

My teachers could see all the welts and bruises, but they never commented—at least, not to me. They only stared at me, sometimes coldly. There were days I was still bleeding when I got to school. My classmates who noticed would laugh and make fun or say, "Oh, you got another beating," as if they thought I must have deserved it. I just ignored them.

If I had on a short sleeve dress or blouse, I draped my sweater around my shoulders to try and hide my arms as much as possible. Putting my arms inside the sweater sleeves was much too painful, and sometimes blood would stick to the sweater to where it was difficult to remove.

SMALL SPACE

Daddy was the one who always went out to find the switches. Even though there were several trees in the empty field across the street from our block of houses, I never knew where he got the ones he found. I was sure he wouldn't go into anybody's yard to take any off their trees. Nevertheless, it always amazed me how he always found so many so easily, even in winter. It was a threatening and unnerving sight when he walked in the house with a handful of them.

When she ran out of switches and Daddy wasn't around to go get any, my stepmother started sending Donnie and me out searching for some. We had no idea where to look and were only able to find dried-up short, scrawny ones. Some were no more than twisted, gnarly twigs. In the summertime, branches were so brittle, they snapped as we tried to break them off a tree. And in the wintertime, they were green and fresh and resisted being cut. Our hands got so cold, we could barely make our fingers work. It was a difficult task trying to find good ones like Daddy found.

But we knew better than to come home empty handed. So we walked around in the open field, searching out all the trees to see if there were some branches we could reach that would be suitable to cut with the dull kitchen knife we had brought with us. We were both so short that we couldn't reach but a few of the very low-hanging branches. The better ones were always too high. We were also hoping nobody saw us.

On one of our trips across the street to the field, breathing in the cool early-morning air—the temperature in the mild eighties—I was musing on what a beautiful Saturday it was. It was much too nice out there to be cutting down switches. I thought we should have been out riding bikes and shooting marbles, not satisfying my stepmother's sadistic appetite for law and order.

As I sawed away at what I hoped was a suitable branch, I tried to imagine a time when I would not have to do any of this—a time when I would not have to endure another beating, a time when I would not have to be afraid, a time when I could play in the backyard with my friend Janice, a time when I would not have to run home from school and check the clock in fear, a time when I could run to my Daddy and hug him and say "I love you" without my stepmother going off the deep end.

Would there ever be such a time? I wondered on that one day, shaking my head wistfully. *It's almost too much to ask for.*

Still, I managed a slight smile, thinking, *Maybe someday, maybe someday. Just keep hoping. Maybe someday.*

Sometimes when she didn't have switches, my stepmother beat us with a broken broom handle that she kept standing in a corner of the living room next to a closet. The first time I saw it, I stared at it in amazement. I wondered where that broken broom handle came from. She nonchalantly told us that she couldn't always wait for Daddy, so she had to find something else to use.

I couldn't imagine being hit with a broom handle. She could kill us if she hit us with that thing. But she did—on our heads, arms and legs, wherever it landed.

Each time she did, each blow caused big knots to form on whatever part of our body she struck. Each time she struck me, I felt as if my bones were breaking. I tried to shield my face and head each time she hit me, so my arms were always battered and bruised and lumpy.

One time she hit me in my head with such force, I actually saw stars and heard birds chirping. I thought to myself, unbelievably, that only happened in cartoons. At times I'd get up off the floor after being knocked down from a powerful blow wondering how I could still be alive.

If Daddy wasn't working late, his usual time to get home was around 6:30 p.m. My stepmother would tell us, "Go outside and greet your daddy. He's worked all day. That's the least you can do."

I was glad when Daddy got home, but we looked so stupid going out just to say *hi* every evening and walking back into the house. I was always trying to find something to do so I wouldn't have to go out there because sometimes kids were out playing and saw us. And the next day at school, they teased us about it.

When Daddy worked in construction, many times he came home so tired that once he sat down in the kitchen chair, he could barely get back up.

"Come and take my boots off and run me some bath water," he would tell one of us kids.

The crew with whom he worked did various construction jobs. Sometimes they paved roads or poured tar all day in the hot sun or they worked on constructing a building in the freezing cold. At times, wincing from exhaustion, it was all he could do to eat a little dinner, climb up the stairs, soak in his hot bath, and fall into bed.

He occasionally brought home debris from his job in the trunk of his car. When it had accumulated to where the trunk was getting too full, he told us kids to go clean it and throw the stuff away because he was always too tired to do it. We went out to the car and opened up the trunk.

Among the clutter were pieces of rubber, wire, bent nails, empty cans of caulking, newspapers, rags splattered with paint, and a hundred other items that made Daddy's trunk a whole world in itself. The stuff we couldn't identify, we asked about so we wouldn't mistakenly throw away an important item he needed on the job. My stepmother demanded to know what we were throwing out, even after Daddy had told us to get rid of it all.

On one of these occasions, we were taking out the usual stuff and came across several pieces of rope that resembled black licorice. As we brought them into the house to ask Daddy if we should throw them out or not, they caught her eye immediately. When Daddy said "You can toss those," she pounced on us like a cat and snatched them away from us.

"Give me those pieces. They'll make good straps," she said excitedly.

Daddy looked at her but didn't respond. She searched out several pieces the length of a belt and decided to keep them.

"Go get me the butcher knife. This piece is too long."

"Yes, ma'am."

She tried to shorten it by cutting it with the butcher knife, but it resisted and only cut partially through. Inside the licorice-like cord were several thin intertwined wires with cotton running through each wire, making it impossible to cut through even with the sharpest knife.

"All right. Throw these out. I'll just keep the two short pieces."

So the longer ones we threw away, but the two shorter pieces she kept because they were just right. These became her favorite weapons and our most feared.

Whether she beat us with the switches, the broom handle, or the strap, they were all very, very painful. But the strap immediately split the skin and drew blood, much more effectively, she said, than the switches did. And if the skin didn't split, the welt it left was usually larger than the one the switch left and sometimes even broke open later.

Off and on at varying times, Daddy worked at a car wash. But for most of our growing-up years, he was in construction. In both jobs, he couldn't work when it rained. In the car-wash business, on rainy days, they closed down, and everybody went home. But in construction, they only quit if the project was outdoors and it rained for hours without letting up.

We kids prayed for rain at the slightest cloud. And even though Daddy didn't help us out when we got in trouble, we were desperate to have him home because just the fact that he was there kept our stepmother from beating us. Yelling we could tolerate, but not the beatings.

If Daddy's company's project was indoors, he'd have to go to work, no matter what the weather. Our hearts sank when that happened.

During the rainy season, when they were working on an outdoor project and the really bad summer storms came, there were times when Daddy would be home for days at a time. We quietly basked in the joy of having him around. Rainy days for us were anything but gloomy. Up in our room, the pitter-patter of the rain on the roof only added to the coziness of the day.

We didn't know how much money Daddy was losing when he couldn't work because we didn't know anything about the finances or about the running of the house anyway—except when we asked for something for school, my stepmother said every time, "Your daddy can't afford to buy you nothing, so don't ask for nothing."

On those days when the weather kept Daddy home, he and my stepmother would sit at the kitchen table for hours, talking and drinking pots of coffee and looking out the kitchen window. We were never included or allowed into their conversations. And if they thought we were listening in, my stepmother would say, "Get out of here and quit listening in. Ain't nobody talking to you."

We went about quietly doing our work and then retreated upstairs to our room—something we couldn't do when Daddy was working. Joe yelled at us when he was home but not as much. And if we did something that she thought warranted a beating, she saved it until he went back to work, which was pretty scary. So we always tried to walk the straight and narrow, even when Daddy was around.

Daddy beat me only a few times in my life. One of the beatings all three of us got from him was for stealing candy bars from Chensue's Market, up the street. We each had gone to the market at different times that week for my stepmother and had taken a candy bar. We had hidden them in our room upstairs, waiting for an opportunity to sneak and eat them, and one of our older brothers found them.

Those candy bars looked so good in that counter. Looking around and seeing no store employee, it was easy to pick one up and walk out the store. Even though my heart raced at the thought of stealing my favorite Big Time candy bar, it looked too easy not to take advantage of the opportunity. And even though Daddy beat us pretty bad, it wasn't nearly as bad as it would have been had my stepmother got a hold of us.

I knew it was wrong to steal the candy, but I wished that they had talked to us and punished us a different way instead of beating us.

One of the other beatings I received from Daddy was when he had gotten home from work one evening and was sitting in the kitchen taking his work boots off. He had recently gotten a new set of false teeth. To which he had been trying to get adjusted. But because they still hurt his mouth, he had worn his old ones to work that day.

"Goatie," as he always called me, "go upstairs and get my teeth off the nightstand."

"Yes, sir."

I ran upstairs, picked up the teeth off the nightstand, and bounded back downstairs. As I was walking into the kitchen and was only a few feet from Daddy, they slipped out of my hand, fell on the floor, and broke in half.

I was shocked. How could I possibly have done that?

"Now you've done it. How could you have done something so stupid?" my stepmother yelled.

"I just bought those teeth. They were brand-new," Daddy said, obviously angry. "Go get the switch."

"But, Daddy," I wailed, "it was an accident. You saw me. I wasn't playing around. I didn't mean to drop them."

"But you shouldn't be so careless," he said. "Go get the switch."

I wanted to run out the door and never come back. Why did I get beaten for everything I did, even when it was accidental? When Daddy beat me, I cried as much from anger and hurt feelings as I did from the beating itself.

I had wanted to run away that night but didn't. I knew I would have to come back anyway. Donnie had more guts than I did, I guess, because he had begun to run away not long before. He never went to anybody's house. He just took off running aimlessly up the street and through the fields. And he was never gone for more than an hour or two because each time he left, I would have to go look for him or Daddy would if he was home.

Al and I always begged him not to go but hoped he would make a successful escape. He never did, and it never took long to find him. And then I'd have to talk him into coming back home.

Daddy was always the one who beat Donnie when he ran away, and my heart would nearly break for him as the switch whooshed through the air as each blow landed on Donnie's back. I felt as if I were being beaten myself. I always cried for him. But getting beaten didn't stop him from running. Al and I tried to convince him that running away wouldn't do any good and would only get him a bad beating, which he didn't deserve.

Joe and Daddy never tried to talk to him to find out what the problem was, why he ran away. They just asked, "Why did you run away?" and his response was always the same—"I don't know."

They never pursued it further. That was the extent of the conversation. He told me he knew it wouldn't help to try and explain, so he didn't. As much as Donnie ran away, Daddy had to know something was wrong.

3

Oatmeal for Breakfast

That stupid pot of oatmeal is simmering on the stove again this morning. I hate oatmeal. Why do I always look hopefully for signs of bacon and eggs? I tell myself as I pass through to the utility room to get the broom.

Did I think anything would ever change? The answer to that question was always no.

My stepmother fixed bacon and eggs and toast for Daddy every morning before sending him off to work. She never asked us kids what we wanted for any meal. She fixed what she wanted to fix. We had oatmeal for breakfast seven days a week. Didn't she ever think that we would have liked something different for a change? There was all kinds of food in the cabinet.

The only morning of the year that was different was Easter Sunday morning when we all ate at the kitchen table together as a family. We couldn't talk at the table, but we didn't care. We were used to my stepmother's rule of not speaking unless spoken to. We don't even think Daddy knew of the rule or noticed us never talking.

On Easter morning, we each had one egg, one piece of toast, and one slice of bacon. Marvelous. We were still hungry, but we were always hungry. It wasn't that we didn't have plenty of food; it's just that we didn't get it and we could never serve ourselves at any meal.

We had never been given seconds, and today was no different. Whatever Joe put on our plates was it, and whether we liked it or not, we had to eat it. That's the way things were. I was used to going to bed hungry. So I was always glad when Easter came—mainly just for the breakfast.

One morning before I went downstairs to retrieve the broom and cleanser, I prayed extra hard, "Please, God, please let us have something besides oatmeal for breakfast. I don't care what it is. Almost anything would be better than oatmeal. I am so sick of it, I could just throw up."

I just knew my prayers would be answered. I also knew by now that even God was sick of oatmeal. I dashed downstairs excited, expecting the aroma of fried potatoes or bacon and eggs. But there it was—that ominous pot of oatmeal staring back at me from the stove, almost mocking me. Back upstairs, hot tears of anger and frustration rolled unchecked down my face. I even felt abandoned by God.

And just when I thought breakfast couldn't get any worse, my stepmother discovered a new recipe on the back of a box of oatmeal that included nonfat dry milk. The recipe called for mixing the dry milk first with water, then adding it to the oatmeal while cooking, making it thick, rich, and creamy.

But she decided to shortcut it and, as the oatmeal cooked, dump the dry powdered milk into it right out of the box without mixing it with water. That way, she said, she didn't have to pour milk on the oatmeal when she served it. It was her way of saving milk, and she used this method every day after that.

Many of the powdery lumps dissolved or broke up in our mouths because the dry milk had not been mixed. Thick and slimy, the oatmeal stuck in our throats. We gagged as we tried swallowing each spoonful. Unable to discuss it at the table, we glanced at one another and tried not to frown as we labored to consume the lumpy mess. And she only put one scant teaspoon of sugar in each of our bowls, so it wasn't even sweet.

She and Daddy ate scrumptiously in the living room in front of the television set every night, except when Daddy was too tired after work so then he ate at the kitchen table. They never ate with us though. The three of us always ate at the kitchen table and talked softly when we could get away with it, got right up and did the dishes, cleaned the stove off, and swept the floor—every night's routine.

She always prepared two meals, one meal for us and another for her and Daddy. Daddy had mouthwatering dinners like pork chops and rice or salad and Pepsi, while we had beans and cornbread or greens and cornbread or rutabagas, which I hated. She laid the cornbread in the middle of the liquid from the greens or beans on the plate. The bottom of the cornbread was usually burnt.

Milk or salad at mealtime for us was nonexistent. We only indulged in those precious foods at Aunt Tick's house. Daddy's food always smelled so good that my mouth watered.

For Thanksgiving and Christmas dinner, Daddy moved the kitchen table into the middle of the living room, and we actually ate turkey and dressing dinner together on the holidays.

Once incurring her wrath for not finishing one of my chores, after she had put dinner on my plate, my stepmother wouldn't allow me to eat until Donnie and Al had eaten. I had to sit at the table and watch them eat, not allowed to touch my food. Then we washed the dishes and swept the floor. By then, mine was completely cold.

"That kitchen better be clean," she growled at me from the living room.

"Yes, ma'am. It's clean. We're finished."

"Now you got exactly one minute to eat your dinner."

I hurriedly sat down at the table and began to gulp down my cold food, trying not to look like a pig as I ate, not wanting to incite her wrath more. Sitting in her chair in the living room like a vulture on a perch, her eyes became narrow slits as she stared in the kitchen at me with obvious hatred on her face. It was almost impossible to eat with her glaring menacingly at me and the clock during that one minute. I almost choked trying to get the food down.

Daddy, where are you? Please come home, I prayed.

With Daddy not being home from work yet, I knew she would beat me if I didn't finish in exactly one minute. I finished just barely.

Avoiding her angry gaze, I got up from the table and quickly washed my plate. I felt her icy stare follow me as I eased past her upstairs. I held my breath, hoping not to get hit or kicked as I passed her.

In one of my stepmother's rare pleasant and talkative moments, I seized the opportunity to inform her that I didn't like raw onions. I told her I didn't like onions—period. But I had never had the nerve before to tell her. Sometimes she chopped onions up on greens, and I didn't like them at all. But I thought then that maybe while she was in a good mood, she would accept it. I would just start with the raw ones. But that was a big mistake. Her whole countenance changed.

"What do you mean you don't like onions? How can you like cooked onions and not like raw onions?" she said.

"I don't know," I said timidly. "The cooked ones don't taste as strong as the raw ones. The raw ones taste bitter."

I hadn't expected her to get angry over onions.

"Well, if you stay in this house, you gonna eat them. I never heard of anything so stupid. You've eaten them up to now and you never said nothing. How can you like them one way and not the other? You don't know what you like."

She kept shooting questions at me, not waiting for answers. I stood quietly until she finished her tirade and then slipped out of her sight. She fumed about onions on and off for years after that. I never expressed my likes or dislikes about anything again.

Unlike other kids, we didn't look forward to our birthdays—in fact, we dreaded them. The last thing we needed around that house was a birthday. The birthday itself came and went. And regardless of what day of the week the person's birthday fell on, she didn't make the cake until the following Sunday.

Except for hers and Daddy's, it was a nuisance to her that there was another for which birthday she had to bake. She only wanted to make cakes when she felt like it. And it just so happened, our birthdays never came around when she felt like baking.

Whosoever birthday it was had more chores on their birthday and the Sunday that she made the cake and most of the cleanup after the cake was baked. That person was also fussed at and yelled at the most that day also because my stepmother blamed them for the extra work involved in making their cake.

There were no birthday presents or parties for any of us. We all stood around the table and sang a lifeless "Happy Birthday" song as she let the birthday person cut themselves a small piece of their cake. She cut the other two a small slice each. We savored every bite because we knew we wouldn't get anymore. She sliced and ate off it during the week, and she packed a slice in Daddy's lunch every day until it was gone.

We didn't dare try and steal any of it because we knew it would be too easy to tell if we did. But we did try our hand at stealing sugar. When she bought sugar, she always poured it out of the bag into an empty shortening can that had the label removed. She kept it up in the cabinet over the kitchen sink with a piece of masking tape on it that said "Thou Shalt Not Steal." And even though she never actually caught us and we never admitted it, she knew we were sometimes stealing sugar.

When she and Daddy went to the grocery store or when we knew they would be out of the house for a while, we'd take note of how the sugar bucket was situated, carefully take it down from its second-shelf spot, and each of us would eat a teaspoon of sugar out of it. How sweet it was. We would rather have cake, but that would do.

We were always careful to put the bucket back just the way she had it, although sometimes she accused us of stealing sugar when we really hadn't touched it. She was so paranoid about it, she just forgot how she had left it.

She kept one or two loaves of bread on top of the refrigerator. And occasionally, we stole a slice if we thought she wouldn't be able to tell. But we were careful not to do it too often because there was always a chance of getting caught.

Donnie was as daring in stealing bread as he was about running away. He could climb up on the edge of the chair by the refrigerator and steal a slice while they were right around the corner watching TV, and he'd get away with it. I would be paralyzed with fear watching him while he'd just sneak off with it and laugh.

My stepmother counted the fruit she bought religiously because she said if she didn't, we would steal it, although we had never stolen any before or even wanted to. We'd never steal anything that could be counted so easily. We knew better. We only stole bread and sugar because we were hungry most of the time. She counted practically everything. The fruit she bought was for her and Daddy, and we were not allowed to have any.

However, one dreadful Saturday morning, she had gone back upstairs to get dressed after Daddy had gone off to work. We got up and dressed, and I went downstairs as usual to get the cleaning supplies to start my chores. She came down almost immediately behind me.

For some reason, she opened the refrigerator, counted the peaches, and came out saying that one was missing. And since I had been the only one downstairs, she accused me of taking it.

"Glo, you took one of the peaches out of this refrigerator," she said, standing at the open refrigerator door.

"No, ma'am. I didn't take it," I said, completely surprised, wondering when I was supposed to have taken it.

I hadn't been downstairs long enough to take it, even if I had wanted to, because she came right down behind me. She had to know I didn't take it.

"Go get me that strap," she said. "I told you about stealing."

"But Mama, I didn't do it," I said, my voice trembling and my eyes wide with fear. "I didn't take that peach. Call Daddy at work and ask him if he took it. He probably did."

"I ain't calling your Daddy on his job. And he wouldn't have taken it anyway without telling me."

I felt paralyzed with fear as I went to get the dreaded black strap. She jerked it from me, and she told me to get the footstool that was sitting in the corner in the living room. I pulled the stool from the wall. She pulled a chair from the kitchen into the living room and sat down in it.

"I don't want to have to get up from here either," she told me. "Pull that stool over here and lie across it."

"Please, Mama. Please don't beat me. I didn't take it. I didn't. I promise I didn't."

"Shut up and lay across that stool."

As I lay down across the stool, she brought the strap down hard across my back. Every time I screamed and jumped up, she'd yell, "Get back down there." Over and over again she hit me until my back and arms were bloody.

"Mama, I didn't take it. I didn't take it," I was crying from pain and disbelief.

How could this be happening? She knows I didn't steal that peach. Every time I jumped up, she ordered me back down and kept beating me.

When she finally stopped and told me to get up and put the strap away, I rolled off the stool onto the floor and, with great difficulty, staggered to my feet. My eyes fell on the clock in the living room. She had beaten me for twenty minutes.

She threw the strap at me and walked away. Still sobbing, my clothes disheveled, I stumbled upstairs and went into the bathroom. I tried to button my blouse and tuck it back into my pants, but every part of my body was red hot with pain. And my hands shook so violently, I couldn't get the buttons fastened.

I sat on the side of the bathtub and rested my forehead on the edge of the sink and cried in despair, "I miss you, Mama. I miss you so much."

When Daddy came home, she told him that she beat me for stealing a peach. He gave her a surprised look and said, "I took that peach for my lunch."

"Oh. I didn't know you took it 'cause you didn't say anything. Well, she would have done something else to deserve a beating anyway, so I'm not sorry I did it."

I was relieved to know that Daddy had taken the peach. However, I was looking for him to say something in my behalf, something in my defense, but he didn't say a word. He knew what kind of beatings my stepmother was capable of giving us, but he didn't even look at me.

I was angry. I wanted to take my blouse off and show him how bloody my back and legs were from that black cord. I wanted to scream at him and say, "Look at me, Daddy. Look at how bad she's beaten me for something I didn't even do. Why don't you help me, Daddy? Why don't you help me? Why do you let her beat me like this?"

As usual, though, the wounds had barely started to heal, as the next beating came a few days later.

4

New Shoes

To my surprise, a few days before the beginning of my fifth grade school year, Daddy went out and shopped for me. He didn't take me with him, and I didn't even know he was shopping. But when he came home from the store, I stood mesmerized as he retrieved from the shopping bag a gorgeous black wool coat with a soft white fur collar and a smart-looking pair of low-heeled burgundy shoes with a double strap across the top.

I lovingly caressed the coat. As I slowly ran my hand across the collar, its softness reminded me of a tiny baby kitten, cuddly and soft as a cloud. I carefully hung the coat in my closet. It was to be for church only.

With my new shoes, I would start school in style. I could hardly wait. How did Daddy know what I needed and wanted so badly?

On the first day of school, I stepped into my shoes, a perfect fit. They felt so good and looked so smart. I promised myself I would take good care of them and not get scuff marks on the toes. I proudly wore them all year.

But the next year, I didn't get new shoes. And my once-new shoes were now old shoes and began to get tight on my feet. And then they began to really hurt. They got so tight that when I put them on, I tried to press my heels to the back of the shoes as much as possible in order to allow room for my toes. I also tried curling my toes to keep them from pressing hard against the toe of the shoes. Nothing was working anymore. Then I started to limp and sometimes cry from the pain.

I was afraid to tell my stepmother that my shoes were too small and my feet hurt, but the pain became too great. And when I ventured to tell her, "Mama, my feet hurt," she snapped.

"Your Daddy don't have no money to buy you no shoes!" she yelled.

I couldn't tell Daddy my feet hurt because she had ordered us not to tell him about anything that had to do with money. Clothes, shoes, glasses, and afterschool activities—she considered frivolous. So even though I needed new shoes badly, I knew I couldn't tell him. But I knew he would buy them for me if I could just let him know I needed them.

Even when I was in the first grade, the teacher had sent a note home informing my parents I needed glasses, "Please make an appointment with the school. Your child needs glasses."

My stepmother read the note and said, "You see what you want to see," crumpled it up, and threw it in the trash. And she warned me not to tell Daddy about it or she would get me. I never got glasses, and I was sure Daddy never knew I needed them.

I felt as though I was being punished for growing. I never told any of my teachers I needed glasses because I knew it would do no good to take home another note from another teacher. So every year, I sat near the front of the classroom in order to see the blackboard.

Sometimes my stepmother did what was called daywork, cleaning people's houses for eight dollars a day. The women for whom she worked, when they paid her, also gave her their old clothes and shoes. I don't know if they had sons or not, but they never gave her any boys' clothes, only women and girls. She sometimes rummaged through until she found a dress or two that fit her.

I would have been embarrassed to give anybody some of the stuff they gave her. But she went through the boxes as if they were full of gold nuggets. She didn't seem to notice that most of the clothes were drab, too large, and outdated for her or me. Some even needed extensive mending.

She shoved the skirts and dresses at me and told me, "Go, try these on." Everything was always too big for me. Never once was there an outfit that fit. But when I realized she intended to make me wear them anyway, I quickly learned to be creative and managed to make them fit with belts and safety pins.

But there was nothing I could do with the shoes. There were never any that were the proper size or that even looked nice. Sometimes there was only one shoe. Other times, there would be two or three shoes in the box. They were beat up, old-fashioned, ill fitting, and hurt when I tried them on; and the heels were run down on every pair.

If they happened to be too big, she made me stuff the toe with toilet paper. If they were to small, there was no remedy for that. She said, "You just have to wear them anyway."

Every step I took, sharp pains shot through my toes like small daggers. It was all I could do to concentrate on walking and standing up straight.

"Since you say your feet hurt, wear these to school," she'd say as she handed me a pathetic-looking pair out of one of the boxes. "They're bigger than the ones you got on."

She didn't understand that too big was just as bad as too small. I tried wearing the ones that were too big to school first and found they hurt just as much as the ones that were too small. One day, as I walked down the hall toward my English class, my fifty-four-year-old English teacher, Mrs. Crumpton, was standing in the door, greeting us on our way into the classroom.

Our mouths simultaneously dropped open as we stared at each other's feet. The shoes we had on were identical—only hers looked fairly new, and mine looked like they were ready for the trash heap. Neither of us said a word, but instead of having to pass her and go into class, I wanted the floor to open and swallow me up.

I sat at my desk and pulled my feet under me and tried to hide the hideous shoes by crossing my legs at the ankles, but it was too late.

As the other kids began to notice our shoes, a few of them began to snicker, tap their friends on the shoulder, and point at me. The teacher didn't stop the kids from making fun of me, and she would occasionally look over at my shoes and smile. I couldn't concentrate on any aspect of the lesson that day. Their insensitivity was painful.

But I was more hurt and embarrassed by the teacher's amusement than I was my classmates'.

I used to hear my teachers talking about me and laughing at me in the hallway when they thought I wasn't listening. Sometimes they were as heartless as the students. I felt alienated and alone all the time. I had absolutely no one to talk to.

My teachers are adults, I thought. *If they won't help me, at least don't talk about* me.

Forced to wear those shoes again, I was walking down the hall the next morning past my English class, limping badly. My feet hurt so bad that day, I could barely walk or concentrate. At times, walking from one class to another, pains shot through my toes so bad, I had to stop and lean against the wall until the pain somewhat subsided.

Mrs. Crumpton was again standing outside of her classroom door with another teacher, and they stared disdainfully at me as I passed. I tried to walk a little straighter.

"Why is she limping?" the other teacher asked.

"Oh, she just wants attention," Mrs. Crumpton replied.

I thought I would just die.

My stepmother had me trying on a dress in her bedroom one day that she had gotten out of one of the bags of clothes. I was wearing blue jeans and a blouse, but I didn't have a slip-on underneath the blouse. I was just starting to need a bra, but she hadn't let me wear one yet. Donnie was in the room with us, and when I tried to turn my back away from him, my stepmother wouldn't let me.

"What are you doing?" she said.

"Since Donnie is in here, I'll go in the bathroom and try it on," I said.

"Oh, girl, Donnie is your brother," she said. "He don't care nothing about you. Take off that blouse and try this dress on."

When I took my blouse off, Donnie's eyes got as big as saucers as he stared at my chest. I closed my eyes and flushed hot with anger and embarrassment.

"*Stop looking at me*," I wanted to scream at him. I felt completely violated.

For church, I owned a pair of black patent leather shoes that were off limits for school, and they hurt even more than all the others combined. The insides were hard, they were stiff and didn't bend, and, like my school shoes, had long since gotten too small. So my growing feet had no room to move around in these either.

"Hurry up and get down here. You gonna be late for Sunday school," my stepmother yelled up the stairs at us as we scrambled to grab our Sunday school lessons and run downstairs.

"Bye, Mama. Bye, Daddy," we each called out as we took off out the back door down the steps.

They were both standing on the porch and watched us leave.

Why are they standing outside on a Sunday morning? I wondered briefly.

It was difficult for me to walk normally, and I was trying hard not to let them see me limping. We had only gone about half a block, and I was in such pain that silent tears formed on my eyelids and spilled over onto my blouse.

Donnie noticed me crying.

"Don't cry, Glo, 'cause if you cry, you know Mama's gonna call you back. She's watching us."

"I can't help it," I said. "My feet hurt so bad."

"Girl, come back here," my stepmother barked behind us. "What you crying about and why you limping?"

"My feet hurt," I said sheepishly, unsuccessfully trying to dry the frustrating tears that kept coming.

"Get in that house and put on your school shoes."

Even though Daddy didn't say anything, I was glad he was there. I didn't know what would happen when I got home from Sunday school, but at least I knew she wouldn't hit me while he was standing right there.

I didn't even know which shoes to put on. They all were either too big or too small, and they all hurt. I had four pairs to choose from, and none of them fit. But I had to hurry and change into something and get out of there.

I grabbed one of the pairs that were too big and hurriedly put them on. The toilet paper I had previously stuck in the toes was still there. As I fastened the straps and stood up, pains shot through both feet in numerous places, making it difficult to get down the stairs. I held onto the stair railing and hurriedly made my way back downstairs and outside.

Donnie and Al had walked back to the house with me and were waiting out on the sidewalk. When I got back outside, Joe and Daddy were still standing on the porch and watched me again walk down the sidewalk.

I tried harder than before not to limp, which made the pain even worse. But this time, she didn't call me back. When we turned the corner, Donnie and Al slowed down so I could limp the rest of the way to church.

5

Sunday School

Sunday school and church were mandatory for us. Church attendance was as routine as school attendance. There was not a Sunday growing up that I remember any of us kids missing church and staying home. We missed school sometimes, but not church. Every Sunday—rain or shine, winter or summer—we were there. Even storms or threat of a hurricane didn't keep us home.

It wasn't that we were so spiritual. My stepmother just made us go. She and Daddy never went to Sunday school but always sent us, and then they drove to church later.

Sunday school classes were held in the large basement of our church. The five or six classes were split up into different sections. Each class maneuvered their chairs around so that their backs would be toward the other classes to gain some semblance of privacy. There were so many of us, it was difficult to separate the classes far enough apart not to hear one another. Teachers had to make a concerted effort to teach quietly and maintain order because of the lack of sufficient space.

The walk to Sunday school was quite enjoyable until we reached the church. We walked in and went down the short set of stairs, turned the knob and opened the heavy door leading to the basement.

No matter how slowly we opened the door, the long, agonizingly loud screech was worse than a dozen set of fingernails on a blackboard.

"Why don't they ever oil this door?" I muttered through gritted teeth as I tried to avoid the stares as all heads turned toward the door.

We were late every Sunday, and classes were nearly over by the time we arrived. There were the usual headshakes and looks of disgust on the teachers' faces as they looked from us to the clock. There were smirks from the kids as a few of them leaned over and whispered to one another.

The three of us split up and went to our individual classes, and the teachers included us in the lessons as best they could. Sometimes we were so late and had missed so much already that they didn't even try to include us. Those were the times we wished we could skip Sunday school altogether, but we knew we had to go in. There was no place else to go. And, God forbid, Joe and Daddy ever found out from one of the adults that we weren't there.

Sunday school also started at nine o'clock, just like school did. After we sat down and apologized for being late, our teachers scolded us in front of the other students, reminding us we needed to be on time so we wouldn't miss so much of the lesson. I felt so small. By the sternness of their voices and the stony glares they gave us, I knew it would be futile to try and explain our lateness.

They didn't know that we weren't allowed to leave home until nine o'clock every Sunday morning. Joe didn't think it was important enough for us to be on time for Sunday school, just that we needed to go. The pain of Sunday school and school had started to blend together.

There was one redeeming part about going to Sunday school, though, and that was stopping at the liquor store on the way. Daddy gave us a nickel every Sunday for the offering plate. Once in a while, we actually put our offering in the plate. But many times, if we left home after nine o'clock, we knew we would be too late and would probably miss the offering plate. So we chose to go to the liquor store.

A nickel would buy what was called a grab bag, a small, six-inch paper bag stuffed full with various sorts of wonderful penny candy and twisted at the top to close. Each bag was different. Some bags were fatter than others and sometimes contained more than twenty pieces of candy. Some bags were so full, they couldn't be twisted. They were just sort of pinched together at the top. What a treat it was to walk along and eat and trade candy from each other's bags.

When the store sold out of grab bags, we had to buy a candy bar, which wasn't nearly as special. The owner never talked to us but sometimes stared at us with distrust, as if he knew we were stealing our offering money. He didn't know it was the most food we'd had all week, even though it was candy.

One sunny Sunday morning, we were walking along enjoying our grab bags when I casually spotted a lone car slowly approaching from behind. I wouldn't have noticed except it drove close up to the curb right alongside us.

I felt the blood drain from my face as I recognized Daddy. If he caught us spending our Sunday school money on candy, we would get a beating for sure. He looked right at us and then slowly drove off, disappearing out of sight up the street. We lost our taste for the rest of our candy.

We were downright scared that morning and dreaded going home after church because we knew what punishment awaited us. But to our amazement, Daddy never mentioned the incident to Joe because she would have screamed at us and then beaten us the next day. He also never told us he caught us either, although he knew we saw him. I was grateful to him for saving us from at least one beating.

6

Two Weeks in Hell

Once a year, it happened, just like clockwork.

"Hazel, what you doing?" came the singsong voice of Miss Ida Mae, our neighbor from up the street.

"Go let Ida Mae in," my stepmother called to me one Saturday morning as I was washing breakfast dishes.

"I just came by to say hi and see what you're up to today."

"Oh, nothing."

"You got time to visit a little?

"Yeah. I just put dinner on to cook, so I'm free for now."

Pulling up chairs, they both sat down at the kitchen table. Then as if unveiling a trophy, Ida Mae ceremoniously removed a bottle of whiskey from its paper sack, placing it in the middle of the table.

Leaning over closely as if revealing top-secret information, she almost whispered, "I brought us a little something."

Oh no, I thought, a knot forming in my stomach. *Here we go again.*

"Well, I really haven't had a taste for anything," Joe said, as the smile faded from her face.

Ignoring her, Ida Mae asked for a glass.

Did I detect a little disgust in my stepmother's voice? Did she not want to drink with Ida Mae? Then tell her, "How hard could it be to say no to that bottle?"

Upon retrieving two small drinking glasses from the cabinet, they drank and laughed for at least two hours until they were both slurring their words. Then Ida Mae, standing up a little unsteadily and holding on to the table, left and went home. Sometimes the bottle was empty when she left; sometimes there was a small amount still in it.

Why, I wondered, would anybody come over to drink with my stepmother when nobody liked her or wanted to be around her?

I felt like saying to Ida Mae, "Why would you bring liquor into our house? Don't you know what it does to her? Do you have any idea what we go through here already? Do you know it's ten times worse for us when she's drinking? Would you like to see my back and my legs, Miss Ida Mae?"

This was one of the many neighbors my stepmother tried to keep from coming over to visit by burning cornmeal directly on the fire on top of the stove.

"I don't want to be bothered with these nosy women today. This will keep them out," she also muttered to herself as she put urine in a bucket of water and washed the front porch with it.

That was done to keep anybody from walking up on the porch just in case they got an idea to come over for a visit. The smell from the cornmeal alone was so stifling, it was enough to chase anybody off that even made it up to the driveway. I wondered why she bothered doing all of that since they rarely visited anyway.

Some of our neighbors didn't have telephones and would occasionally come over to use our phone. Joe always got her money up front. She always told them in her dry way, "You not gonna use my phone for free. You owe me a dime."

If they didn't have a dime, they saw to it that she was paid before the week was out or they couldn't use the phone anymore. Those kinds of things ran through my mind as I watched her drinking with one of these same women.

That afternoon when Daddy came home from work, he walked in the kitchen, took one look at the nearly empty bottle still sitting on the table, and his face was clouded in anger. Joe was sitting at the table, still in her housecoat, and her short hair was frizzed and unkempt.

"Hazel, can't you ever say no?" Daddy just lit into her. "Why do you always have to drink when those women come over here with liquor?"

With slurred speech, she attacked back, "I don't need you to tell me when I can drink and when I can't. I'm grown. I do what I want to do. You didn't have to buy it. What do you care?"

"You didn't even bother to put any clothes on today or cook any dinner."

"I didn't feel like dressing. And I'll cook when I get ready."

The argument inevitably heated up from there. Before the evening was over, Daddy had gone out and bought another bottle and then came back and started drinking in front of the TV. That led them on a drinking spree where they both drank practically nonstop for the next two weeks. No matter how I tried to figure it out, I never did understand it.

My stepmother didn't have anywhere to go in the mornings, so she could sleep in if she wanted to. But Daddy worked usually six days a week. He never missed a day from work, but I don't know how he managed to do it when they were drinking.

Every morning, they both woke up with giant hangovers. Sometimes Daddy was so sick, I could hear him in the bathroom throwing up before having to go to work. At night during these drinking bouts, they'd both fall into a drunken sleep, Daddy on the couch and my stepmother in her recliner. We'd remain somewhere close by but out of sight until we were sure they were both asleep.

Then we'd tiptoe off to bed, praying Joe wouldn't wake up in the night and call one of us to go get her a drink of water or find her cigarettes. We fetched water and cigarettes for her every day, whether she was drinking or not. Even if she was sitting in the kitchen, she wouldn't get up to get her own glass of water or her pack of cigarettes off the living room table.

Almost every night during these drinking binges, if Daddy fell asleep first, which he usually did, Joe would make us kids search through his pockets, take out all his money, and give it to her. Sometimes he had twenty or thirty dollars. Sometimes he had only a few bucks. It was hard to get to his money, if he had rolled off the couch onto the floor and the pocket with the money in it was underneath him. But she made us get on our knees and pull Daddy up until we were able to shove our hand into his pockets to search. If she hid the money we found, I'd watch where or she would tell me where to hide it.

The next morning, upon waking, Daddy sat on the couch, looked around to get his bearings, and then checked his pockets to find all his money gone.

"Hazel, where is my money?"

"How should I know? I didn't take it."

"Yes you did. You always taking my money every time I go to sleep. I know how much money I had. I never drink so much that I don't know how much money I got in my pocket."

"Why you always accusing me? You probably drank it up before you came home or spent it at the bar you stopped in."

"I didn't stop in no bar. You better give me back my money."

While they argued, Daddy searched under the cushions on the couch, under the edges of the living room carpet, and on the table by his recliner. He even searched her purse. But she was smart. She never hid his money in her purse. She'd hide it under a flowerpot in the living room or a coat pocket in the hall closet or even in a pair of shoes. She only took the bills, never his change because that was harder to hide.

When Daddy didn't find his money, he stopped to go get dressed so he wouldn't be late for work, still angry. I could hardly wait to secretly slip upstairs behind him and tell him that she had made us steal his money. And then I'd go get it for him or tell him where it was. He should have known I would look out for him. I always did. I never felt guilty because Joe had no business stealing it or making us steal it in the first place.

She was just livid every time he found it. But never once did she suspect me of having told him. I knew Daddy needed his money. And if she kept it, she would only use it to buy more liquor.

The first day of her drinking bouts started my trips to Miss Sadie's house, which was the only time I saw Miss Sadie all year. Since I was the oldest, I was the one who always had to go. I remember going to Miss Sadie's house as far back as the fourth or fifth grade. I never went for Daddy, and never did I ever go when he was home.

But he knew about my trips over there. My stepmother never went to Miss Sadie's house. I don't know if she had ever even met her.

Miss Sadie's name was synonymous with bootleg whiskey, even to those who didn't drink or didn't buy from her. Some people didn't buy from her, only because they were afraid of getting caught by the police. Several took that chance because she was cheaper than the liquor store.

My stepmother sent me to Miss Sadie's for whiskey, sometimes two or three times a day. She never invited me into her house, only to the front door where she would open the screen just wide enough to hand me a half pint of whiskey in a brown bag. I'd give her the $1.50, take the bag, and leave.

I don't know if I was curious or just plain nosy, but at times when I knocked on her door, I tried to strain my neck and focus my eyes to see inside the living room. But it was always too dark in there. And she never opened the door wide enough for me to be able to slip inside. I used to wonder what the inside of her house looked like.

I didn't know much about Miss Sadie, just that she had a dark complexion and was heavyset like my stepmother and appeared to be in her forties, although that was only a guess. And she was always nice to me. I rarely saw her outside. And even when she did come out, the times that I saw her, she quickly retreated back into her house. So I never got a chance to really talk to her.

Miss Sadie fussed about Joe sending me so many times a day to her house because she said I was too young to be buying whiskey. But what she was really afraid of was that I would be stopped by the police or I'd unknowingly lead them to her house.

"Who's at your house, child?" she'd say to me.

"Nobody, ma'am. It's just Mama and us kids."

"Where is your daddy?"

"Daddy's at work."

"You don't have company? Who's drinking all this whiskey?"

"Mama is."

"How can Hazel drink so much whiskey all by herself? You sure you not having no company today?"

"Yes, ma'am. I'm sure."

Miss Sadie lived about five miles from us. So when I was sent to her house, I would leave the house, run down to the corner, and watch for cars as I ran across the street to the open field, the same place Donnie would go when he ran away and the same place we went to get switches. Then I'd watch for traffic again as I crossed Middlebelt Road, the main highway that ran by our house, and then down residential streets to get to her house. I ran most of the way and never stopped to talk to anybody. I passed so many houses, and I used to wonder how many people saw me running and how many knew where I was going.

Many times I had to go get whiskey before I left for school in the morning, going as late as nine o'clock when classes were just starting. I'd run as fast as I could across the field stumbling and nearly falling, frustrated because I knew I wouldn't get to school until nine o'clock or later, and that meant another series of lies to my teachers about why I was late.

Miss Sadie was really angry when I'd show up on school mornings. I'd have to knock hard before she'd come to the door. Sometimes it took her so long to answer the door that my knuckles would be sore from knocking. There were times I knew I woke her up with my persistent knocking because when she opened the door, her eyes were still clouded with sleep and she was still in her nightgown and robe. Sometimes she still had a rag tied around her head.

"Child, what you doing over here so early? Ain't you supposed to be in school?"

"Yes, ma'am, I am. But Mama told me I had to come and get her some whiskey before I go to school."

Her face slightly softened as I began to cry.

"Here, wipe your face," she said to me as she momentarily left the door and came back with a damp washcloth. I wiped my face and gave her the cloth back, I but kept crying.

"What is wrong with Hazel? She know it's wrong to be sending you over here so much, especially making you so late for school. What you supposed to tell your teachers?"

"I don't know, ma'am."

And I really didn't because each time I was late, I had to make up a different story. None of my stories or excuses sounded plausible, even to me. It wasn't easy coming up with something different because no matter what I told my teachers, it couldn't be the truth. Miss Sadie knew that I would never tell on her. In spite of what she did, she was well known and people still protected her.

Although they never confronted me, I was sure none of my teachers were ever fooled by any of the excuses I gave. I lied to them because my stepmother either told me to or because telling them the truth would get me into trouble with her. But if she caught any of us in a lie that she had not instructed us to tell, we were beaten viciously.

Some days when I arrived at school late and was trying to give an excuse to one of my teachers, they would look at my arms or down at my legs and see all the old wounds healing up or fresh ones just inflicted and just tell me to go to my seat.

One day while at Miss Sadie's house, I had the $1.50 for the whiskey folded up tightly in my hand, a dollar bill and two quarters. As I stood on the porch, waiting for her to open the door and hand me the bag, the tight little packet fell out of my hand on the porch.

Before I could bend down and grab it, it continued to fall between the weathered wooden slats of the porch about eight inches to the ground below. Since the slats were only about half an inch apart, there was no way to reach a hand in or retrieve it without pulling up the boards of the old wooden porch.

Miss Sadie must have thought I was clumsy to have dropped it. And even though she could see it through the slats, she wouldn't give me the whiskey.

I begged her to let me have it so I wouldn't get in trouble. I told her Joe would be furious with me if I didn't bring it back.

I didn't know if Miss Sadie knew about our treatment at home, but she didn't soften. I even promised her I would run right home and get the money. But she still refused and sent me home empty-handed.

What am I going to do? I agonized, as I left running down the street toward home, looking all around in desperation as if the money were going to fall out of the sky right in front of me and I would trip over it.

When I reached the house and told my stepmother what happened, I was so frightened—I just knew she was going to beat me.

"You think I got money to throw away?" she screamed at me. "How could you drop money under somebody's porch? How do I know you didn't spend it?"

"You can call Miss Sadie, Mama," I hurriedly explained. "You can ask her because Miss Sadie could see it through the porch. I tried to grab it before it went through the slats, but I couldn't, and it fell too far down to reach it. It's still there. You can see it."

Even though she was furious and I was already late for school, she made me go back again with another $1.50. Normally, I would have gotten a beating; but I figured she just didn't have time because I still had to go back over there, come back, and then go to school.

This time, I didn't even try to stop the tears. Not only was I mad at my stepmother, but I was even madder at myself for dropping the money.

Impatiently knocking on the door for the second time now, this time, Miss Sadie just shook her head and handed me the whiskey. I figured she was expecting me to come right back.

Looking down, I could see the money, still in a little packet between the slats. Every time I went over after that, I could see it. It was always there. As far as I know, nobody ever retrieved it.

Except for the time she made us eat newspaper when she wasn't drinking, one of the reasons our fear was so great when Joe drank is because she did things to us that she didn't remember later.

While cooking a big pot of greens for dinner one day, she had a small pot of leftover ones that she had me heating up for her lunch. She had mixed up salt, black pepper, and red pepper in a saucer and sat it on the table.

"Glo, dump that saucer of seasonings in the little pot of greens on the stove," she yelled at me from upstairs.

"Mama, don't you mean the big pot?" I said.

"No, I don't mean the big pot. I mean the little pot."

I knew that was wrong, but I always got in trouble if I didn't do exactly what she said. So against my better judgment, I poured the contents of the saucer into the little pot.

Later on, when she came downstairs to eat the greens in the small pot, after the first taste, she knew right away what I had done. They were much too salty to eat.

"Girl, I thought I told you to put that seasoning in the big pot."

"No, ma'am. You said put it in the small pot," I said, and I knew I was in trouble.

"Now what sense would that make? You don't listen to nothing I tell you to do."

I was surprised she didn't beat me.

One evening as we were in the kitchen washing dinner dishes, she came in with a pack of cigarettes in her hand.

She opened the pack and handed us each a cigarette and said, "Now eat it."

She had been drinking heavily that day, but she wasn't drunk yet. She was just at the point where she was mean and nasty and had been spewing out foul, obscene words at us throughout the day, even when we just passed by her.

We each held the cigarette and looked at her in disbelief. She couldn't really be making us eat these cigarettes.

"What you waitin' for? I said eat it."

Biting off a small portion of the cigarettes, we frowned involuntarily as we reluctantly chewed tobacco and cigarette paper together. Each of us began gagging uncontrollably.

"Eat it. And you better not throw it up."

I tried to chew a little at a time and swallow, but I gagged loudly and had to fight back tears and the overwhelming urge to throw up.

"Keep eating."

Her breath reeked with alcohol as she got close to each one of us with a sadistic look on her face, daring us to throw it up. We kept eating, gagging, and choking with each swallow until we had each eaten a whole cigarette.

Chewing on his last piece, Donnie couldn't hold his down, as hard as he had tried. Clutching his stomach, he began to violently throw up.

"I told you not to throw it up, didn't I?" she shrieked, as she reached inside the living room and grabbed a switch out of the corner and began savagely beating him on his head and back while he continued to throw up on the kitchen floor.

Al and I just knew she would attack us next, even though we had managed not to throw ours up—at least, not yet. But we came so close to it. We couldn't stop gagging even after we had swallowed the last piece.

After beating Donnie, she made him clean up the floor. Al and I, still gagging, got paper towels to help him. She had beaten him so badly, we just couldn't leave him to clean up all by himself. She went and sat in the living room and watched us.

Then when we had finished, she told us all, "Get out of my sight."

It was a horrible scene. We all ran upstairs as fast as we could, each one trying to reach the toilet first.

The next morning before she began drinking, she told me to go find her pack of cigarettes.

Realizing I was treading on dangerous ground, I asked softly, "You mean the pack we ate out of last night?

"What you talking about?"

"You made us eat a cigarette out of your pack yesterday."

"No, I didn't," she seethed, her tone menacing.

"Yes, ma'am. You gave us each a cigarette and told us to eat it."

"I never did no such thing, and you know it," she said, lowering her voice. "You just making that up."

As a surge of fear swept through me, I figured I better quit before she got really mad. It was obvious she had no memory of what she did to us.

And so it went from bad to worse with her horrendous forms of punishment and then her lapses of memory concerning them. We tried to make ourselves invisible even more so when she was drinking because when she slanted her eyes and gave us her evil look, we never knew what was going to happen.

The next night, she was at that same evil stage of drinking, sitting in her recliner in her housecoat. She had not bothered to comb her hair all day again, and she was in a particularly foul mood. Daddy had fallen asleep on the couch again.

She told me to go get the shovel from the utility room. Puzzled, I went and got the shovel, wondering what she was going to do with it. She called Donnie to come and stand by her chair.

When I came back with the shovel, she said, "Now hit Donnie on his feet with it."

"No, ma'am," I said incredulously. "You don't want me to do that."

Donnie was barefoot.

"I said hit him on his feet with that shovel!" she screamed when I hesitated.

When I raised the shovel and came down hard with it on Donnie's foot, he jumped up and down and screamed in pain, grabbing his foot.

"Now hit the other one."

I hit the other one. He screamed again and tried to run.

"Come back here," she yelled at him. "Hit him again."

I hit him twice on each foot. I had no choice but to do it. But with each blow, I cringed inside, it hurt me so bad. Donnie hadn't done anything to anger her.

"Now go put that shovel up."

Afterward, I went upstairs and cried with Donnie and tried to console him as he sat on the bed, holding his feet. He pushed me away. I could see the long, angry red marks across the tops of both feet. When he said "You didn't have to hit me so hard," it was as if a knife went through my heart. I felt as if I had been hit with that same shovel. At that moment, I hated myself for not standing up to her.

I was so ashamed that I couldn't get it out of my mind. And for years, every time I thought about it, I would close my eyes and grit my teeth, hearing his screams all over again. I could still see those long red marks. I recall the incident as if it were yesterday.

Then one day, as adults, I could no longer take it. I called Donnie up long distance and recounted the story to him. And even though I was embarrassed, I asked him if he could possibly find it in his heart to forgive me. He laughed and said he had forgotten all about it and was surprised I still remembered it. He also said he bore no scars on his feet at all.

How could he have forgotten that? It was ingrained in my mind forever. But I was relieved that he was willing to forgive me.

7

Daddy's Talks

Saturday and Sunday afternoons was Daddy's time to relax. Sitting in his recliner and reading the newspaper, he kind of zoned out and watched TV after a tough week at work. I felt mentally relaxed just knowing he was home. He was my invisible shield against my stepmother's wrath.

Occasionally, when there was nothing interesting on TV, he'd call me over to his chair and give me one of his talks. I tried to avoid them as often as possible, but he usually caught me off guard when I wasn't thinking about it.

Every chance Joe got, she complained to him about how lazy I was and that she had to keep on me all the time to get my chores done, which was absolutely not true. But she knew I wouldn't dare defend myself for fear of retaliation the next time Daddy left the house. So since he never heard from me, he believed her.

He saved all these things up in his mind for when he had some time to talk to me, as he put it, which turned out to be at least once every month.

We kids kept the house spotless and never gave it a chance to get dirty. The neighbors were always complimenting my stepmother on how immaculate our house was. They'd say things like "How can you have all these kids and have such a clean house? You can eat off the floor."

We heard that a lot.

And then she would embarrass us by saying, "These kids are lazy. They don't do that much. I have to get on them all the time for something. They wouldn't do nothing if I didn't constantly stay on them."

The truth was, the more we did, the more she expected of us. We worked hard daily just to keep her in a good mood, which was tough. The better her mood, the less she yelled and beat us. She reminded us constantly of how much she gave up to come and take care of us. She said many times that if it weren't for us kids, she could have kept her job at the train station or married her handsome boyfriend.

Standing at the side of Daddy's chair, I listened to him repeat all my transgressions and never responded except to say "Yes, sir" and "No, sir." If Daddy could only read my mind and see the truth.

Joe was in the kitchen and heard Daddy call me. She began cursing and noisily slamming dishes and pots and pans around. She didn't like these talks any more than I did, but for different reasons. I always wondered why she complained to him about me if she didn't want him to talk to me.

"I don't know why you wasting your time talking to her," she would say to the stove. "It won't do no good. She ain't never gonna amount to nothing. She just lazy and stupid."

The stove didn't answer.

Daddy, I'm your child. You know I'm not lazy and stupid. Why don't you tell her? I could only say this to myself as I nervously stood there, clasping my hands tight in front of me, wishing he would hurry up and finish.

I was looking at him, but my mind was on the noise coming from the kitchen. I could hear him say, "When you see the dishes need washing, go wash them. Don't wait for her to have to tell you. Sweep the floor. Take out the trash. Do stuff on your own without having to be told. Fix yourself up. Dress like you care about yourself. Hazel cares a lot about you kids. She just wants you to do your best."

Now that was a laugh. That just told me how little Daddy knew of what was going on around there. On and on he went about everything I was already doing. He had no idea what he was saying.

Oh, Daddy, if you only knew, I moaned to myself, *you wouldn't be lecturing to me now.*

I squeezed my hands together tighter as Joe's yelling got louder. Then after about fifteen or twenty minutes, he would finally say, "Well, that's enough for now. You better go help her in the kitchen. She sounds like she's probably mad."

Now why would Daddy send me in the middle of that? The last place I needed to be was in that kitchen. I might as well have been walking into hell itself. Treading softly into the kitchen as if my footsteps would trigger more anger, I was hesitant to say anything to her.

And even though I knew I sounded stupid, I asked timidly, "Mama, is there anything I can help you do?"

She ignored me. When she finally calmed down enough to stop slamming things around, she asked me, "What did your Daddy say to you?"

And after I'd tell her what I could remember, she'd get mad all over again at both of us. I purposely left out the part about how much she cared about us. I always had the fear that her anger concerning Daddy's talks would spill over into the next time he left the house.

I felt I must have been the cause of her unhappiness, and it made me feel guilty. Why else would she beat me so much? I received far more beatings and punishments than Donnie and Al did. I was bruised all the time. And why couldn't she stand for Daddy to talk to me? She practically flew into a rage every time he approached me about anything, no matter how innocuous. So I learned to avoid him as much as possible. I was afraid to even look at him when she was around.

I loved Daddy and I wanted to hug him and show him affection, but I didn't dare. It would cost too much. I ached to sit down and talk to him about school and to ask him questions about Mama. I wanted to tell him how much I missed her.

My stepmother's resentment and jealousy toward me grew more pronounced as I got older, and I grew more fearful of her. There was no place to hide once her anger was turned toward me.

Not long after she came to live with us, I had made the comment that I was going to marry my Daddy when I grew up. I didn't know anything about marriage at six or seven years old. But my perception of Daddy as a child was that there was no other man as perfect as he was, so why not just marry him?

"Explain it to me. If you didn't mean it, why did you say it?" she grilled me about it long after I had already forgotten that I said it.

She always brought it up when she was drinking, which frightened me even more than it did at other times. I never could give her an answer that she was satisfied with.

One evening sitting in our bedroom doing my homework, I could hear Daddy's footsteps coming up the stairs. Since we never talked, I was just going to smile at him. When he reached the top of the stairs, I looked up to see him stop in the hallway.

He just stood there looking at me as if he wanted to tell me something but couldn't get the words out.

Feeling as though I understood, I got up from the dresser and walked up to him and put my arms around him. We hugged each other for a long moment, never saying a word. I wanted to cry but didn't. I just savored the moment. Then he turned and went back downstairs.

Without words, we had silently communicated to each other, "I love you."

That was in junior high. I never remember him hugging me again. Had my stepmother seen us, it would have been the end of me. But she would never steal this moment from me because I kept it in my heart and never told anyone about it.

Mr. Kimble was one of Daddy's friends who lived close by and often came by on the weekends to visit him. I thought he was such a nice man because he laughed loudly and was jovial all the time.

Knowing my stepmother watched me like a hawk whenever one of Daddy's friends came around, I tried to busy myself when he or anybody else visited. But if Mr. Kimble saw me, he never failed to compliment me. He'd look at me as if I were something good to eat.

"Girl, you gettin' prettier and prettier every time I see you," Mr. Kimble said one time.

I mumbled a thank-you while avoiding his gaze.

"What grade you in now?"

"Ninth," I said.

Every year he asked me my age and what grade I was in. I don't know if he really didn't remember or if he was just making conversation. And then he would tell Daddy, "Man, you better watch out for the fellas. Somebody gonna snatch her up. You gonna have to get the shotgun out."

Daddy would just laugh. My stepmother's jaw would be set firm in distaste, never laughing or saying anything. She always jumped on me after he left, saying that I was throwing myself at him because I had smiled and said "Thank you."

8

Three O'clock, School's Out

Fifteen minutes. That's all the time we had—fifteen minutes to get to school and fifteen minutes to get home. My stepmother's intent was to time our arrival home every day once school started, so she had made us walk the distance long ago in the summer.

The elementary school and the high school were both close to our house, only a few blocks away. So fifteen minutes was plenty of time to get to either one. But since that walk was taken in the summertime, there was no one else on the sidewalk but us. We forgot that when school started, there would be hundreds of kids going the same way at the same time, and we had failed to allow for that.

Very few had cars, so we all crowded the sidewalks to get to school. And when school let out, we all crowded the sidewalks to get home. Laughing and talking with their friends, most kids walked more leisurely going home than they walked to school. It was impossible to get around large groups without stepping off the sidewalk into the street.

Sometimes when I walked home behind a group of girls who knew me, as soon as they knew I was behind them, they slowed down, purposely blocking my path. So I had to either choose to stay behind them and risk being late getting home or step off the sidewalk into the street. I would always choose to step into the street.

Then I would hear, "Watch her run."

To their delight, I stepped off the sidewalk into the street around them and broke into a jog, totally humiliated when they started to laugh at my back. But if I was late—I would get a beating for sure.

I wouldn't stop running until I rounded the corner to my house. Then stopping to catch my breath, I would walk normally. Joe got mad if she saw us running, telling us that fifteen minutes was more than enough time to get home and we had no reason to run.

As soon as I entered the house, the first thing I did was look up at the clock on the kitchen wall. If it was 3:15 p.m., I could breathe a sigh of relief. I was safe. But if I was even a minute late, I had to explain why so I wouldn't get beaten. No matter where she was in the house, Joe always knew what time it was. I didn't dare say anything if I was late because then it was worse.

If I walked in the door at 3:14 p.m., she would ask, "Why can't you get home every day at 3:14 p.m.?"

Donnie and Al went through the same thing, even though we were all in different grades. We got out at slightly different times, but we still all had fifteen minutes to get home because we went to the same area of schools.

I often had to do some fast talking to keep her from going to the closet to get the strap, the switch, or the broom handle. Then as my brain raced to come up with a good excuse, my reason would always be because the teacher let us out late. It was usually true, although I was sure we were the only ones who had to bolt from the classroom and run home.

Other times, nothing worked, especially if I was five minutes late. Being that late produced a serious beating. There were times when I had no idea why I was late because I always came straight home, and I did my best to make it on time. Sometimes, things happened that were totally out of my control. And I couldn't tell her that the other kids blocked my path. That wouldn't make any difference.

After checking the clock, the next thing was to check the front of the cabinet door where the dishes were kept. She wrote out a list of chores and taped it to the door for us to see every day. Our name would be put beside our chore unless it was standard and we already knew whose job it was. Her reasoning for doing this was so she wouldn't have to talk to us.

We then went immediately to change out of our school clothes, put on our work clothes and did our chores. We couldn't go outside and play after school, even if we finished. Everything had to be completed before our homework, which we then worked on until dinnertime and finished afterward. Everything in our lives was stiff and regimented.

The junior high school I attended was, thankfully, far enough away to where going home for lunch was impossible. It was a relief to finally take a sandwich to school and not have to go home and eat last night's leftovers. It also saved me from having to check the clock at lunchtime because even though we didn't do chores at noon, we still had the same fifteen minutes to get home.

A block before reaching the school was a train crossing where freight trains ran on dual tracks periodically throughout the day. Caution was required crossing the tracks due to the speed of the trains, and there was no other means for a large number of us to reach the school.

On the first day of school, the principal saw to it that fliers were put in the hands of each student, informing us that even though the trains appeared to be going slowly, they actually were moving much faster than perceived. The flier warned us about the dangers of playing on the tracks and that anyone caught throwing rocks at the trains or walking along the tracks unnecessarily would be disciplined or suspended.

Still, some couldn't resist the temptation to throw rocks at the oncoming trains as they crossed on their way to school in the early morning hours. There were numerous complaints to the school from the railroad authorities about the rock throwing.

There was a very dangerous game we called "chicken" where the object of the game was to stand in the middle of the tracks and wait until the train got perilously close and then dash across the tracks without being struck by the train, a game only a few had nerve to play.

During one afternoon recess, an adventurous group of students ran down to the tracks to play chicken. No train in sight, they threw rocks and laughed as they chased one another back and forth across the tracks. Far off in the distance came the mournful sound of the train whistle. Jumping off the tracks, they waited excitedly. Soon they could see the big hulk of the massive engine roaring heavily down their way.

Thinking that would be a piece of cake, four of them jumped onto the track. Seconds later, when it began to close in on them, no one knows how close it got, but three were able to jump off. One of the girls in the group misjudged how fast the train was really coming and was struck and instantly killed, her body thrown several hundred feet into a ditch.

The news reached the school in minutes. We all rushed inside our classrooms to hear the announcement over the PA System.

"I regret to inform you that one of your classmates has just been struck and killed by a train at the track," it was announced.

We all sat stunned, and then everybody started to cry. There was no use in trying to study or do any work for the rest of the afternoon. Everyone was numb with shock and deeply saddened by the tragedy. We were instructed to remain in our classes until released to go home. We were all crying and hugging one another. Even teachers lost their composure.

When the bell finally rang to end the day, all teachers instructed everyone to gather in the schoolyard. Once outside, the principal expressed his great sorrow for the tragedy and announced that due to the investigation that was beginning at the track, the police would not be allowing us to cross the tracks to go home. So if we would all take different routes home just for that day, he would appreciate it. He apologized for the inconvenience, but he was sure we all understood.

Some students lived in the opposite direction and never needed to cross the tracks, but those of us who did now had to figure out a way to get home. Some were able to make phone calls for parents or a brother or sister to come and pick them up. Those of us who couldn't get rides home had to walk, some a very long way around. I was one of them.

I cringed just thinking about the route I had to take and how long it was going to take me. It was definitely way out of my way. There would be no sense in trying to run it. It was much too far. And even though I walked at a brisk pace, it took me nearly three hours to get home that evening.

In spite of the tragedy that just occurred, I rather enjoyed the long, quiet walk. I watched the cars whiz past me,—obviously moms and dads on their way to pick up their kids from school or others going home, oblivious to what had just happened. I passed a stately weeping willow tree, its long, drooping limbs appearing to be in mourning.

"You can help me mourn for the student we just lost," I told it.

I chuckled as I walked under the viaduct, calling out, "Hello, is anybody in here?" just to hear the hollow, echoing sound that reverberated all around me.

I thought about the girl who had just gotten killed. I didn't even know her, but I felt sorry for her and her family. Did they love her? Would they miss her? Would they miss her as much as I missed my Mama for all these years? I wish I had known something about her. I wish she had been my friend so I could say I lost a friend instead of just saying someone died at school that I didn't know.

Refusing to think about my stepmother up to now, the closer I got to home, the tighter the knot in my stomach got. I didn't know how I was going to be able to explain to her why I was late without her beating me or slapping me. Hopefully by the time I get home, she would have heard something about the tragedy on the radio or the television.

Cautiously stepping in the front door, she was standing there in the kitchen with fire in her eyes.

"Where have you been?" she yelled.

I stayed near the door so she couldn't hit me, as I got the story out as fast as I could, my words almost tumbling over my tongue.

"Mama, I'm late because a girl got killed at school, and they wouldn't let us come home the regular way, so I had to walk all the way down by the viaduct."

"You know you lyin' about being late," she shrieked. "How could you make up a lie like that? You just don't want to get a beatin'. You better tell me where you really been. You ain't never been this late."

She reached for me, but I jumped back in the doorway.

"No, Mama. It's true. Watch the news. It's on TV."

"I don't believe a word of it. You could have made up something better than that."

But to my surprise, she went and turned on the TV, and it was already on the news.

Thank you, Lord, thank you, I prayed, for miraculously she didn't beat me.

"Well, I still don't know why it had to take you three hours to get home."

She just couldn't let up. I stood still, my heart still pounding, wondering if I was supposed to answer that.

I breathed a sigh of relief when she said, "It's too late to change your clothes. Go on upstairs and start your homework."

She never uttered a word of sorrow or remorse for the girl or her family. She never even asked me what happened or whether I knew her. What if that girl had been me, I wondered. She wouldn't have cared at all. She might have even been glad. I was so disgusted—at that moment, I almost wish it had been me.

I really hate you, I fumed to myself. *You don't care about anybody.*

I wished I could tell her how mad I was with her. The anger that began to boil up inside me took over and replaced the anxiety and stress of the situation. And the fact that I did not get a beating did not lessen my contempt for her and her callous attitude.

The students who had been playing chicken that day were suspended. Nobody had the nerve or the desire to play on the tracks for the remainder of the school year.

Since I only attended that school for one year, the next year, I was back to start high school close to home.

Tommy periodically sent us boxes of all kinds of school supplies that my stepmother would make last for months. When the boxes came, as she opened them, we stood by, hungrily eyeing all the neat notebooks, pens, pencils, and crayons. There was so much stuff, we wished we could just take what we wanted. But she rationed out to us five sheets of paper apiece and one pencil each. Sometimes we used all the paper up in one day. And we didn't dare lose a pencil.

When our paper ran out, we borrowed from other kids in our classes, even though there was still plenty at home. Whenever we asked Joe for more paper or another pencil, we had to explain what we had done with the last five sheets or how we could possibly have lost a pencil. Sometimes the kids we borrowed from got mad because we begged so much, especially when we rarely paid back. And some refused to loan us any more.

During football season, Fridays were all abuzz with talk of the upcoming after-school games. I wanted so much to stay and be a part of the crowd and attend a game. Lively pep rallies in the auditorium resounded outside on campus. Everybody was hyped up and excited. But I wasn't allowed to stay after school for anything.

My stepmother said I didn't need to go to the games because they didn't need me and nobody cared whether I was there or not. To me, it wasn't a matter of anybody caring whether or not I was there; I just wanted to go and be a part of the fun stuff that was going on at school.

School was difficult in other ways. I was only allowed to wear two dresses a week to school, one on Monday, Tuesday, and Wednesday and another one Thursday and Friday. My stepmother said she didn't want to do all that washing and that two dresses a week was enough to ruin. I envied the other girls in my classes who wore nice dresses to school, a different one every day. Most of them also wore nylons.

She went in my closet and picked out my school clothes every day. She also combed my hair in the morning before going to school, even in high school. As soon as I rounded the corner on my way to school, I would stop and take the ribbons off and pin the braids up over my head or tie them together in the back so the kids wouldn't laugh at me.

On the way home, I took my hair down again, hoping as I hurried along that I could get it to look the same as how she had combed it in the morning because she sometimes commented that it looked different when I got home.

Janice occasionally came over in the morning to get me so we could walk to school together. Once in a while, she came right at the time my stepmother was combing my hair.

"Don't you know how to comb your own hair?" she asked one time, laughing.

"Yeah," I would retort.

"No, she don't, Janice. She act like she can't do nothing for herself. If I don't comb her hair, she would go out of here looking a mess," my stepmother would say.

On the way to school, I would try and redeem myself with Janice. But she couldn't understand why my stepmother wouldn't let me comb my own hair or wear nylons. I longed to wear my hair curled, nice skirts, and blouses; but that was just a dream. I wanted to look nice like the other girls.

It would have been so pleasant to be able to walk home leisurely and not have to rush out of class, to come home without a knot in my stomach from fear of not knowing what to expect when I got there. And now that I was in high school, the luxury of taking my lunch again was out of the question.

Some of the braver high school kids gathered in little groups at lunchtime. And when they were sure there were no teachers or principal around, they sneaked around to the side of the school and smoked cigarettes. Getting caught smoking meant suspension, which seemed to make it all the more exciting. The "in" groups were always the ones who tried and usually got away with doing daring things.

I wanted to do something cool like trying smoking. I admired them for being so brave. One Sunday morning, as I was helping my stepmother get ready for church, I got my chance. She had gone in the bathroom and left a cigarette burning in the ashtray on the dresser.

Now is my chance, I thought.

I hurriedly laid the dress on the bed I had taken from her closet, took her shoes out and set them on the floor by the bed, and took her nylons out of the drawer and placed them next to her dress. Then I retrieved one of the white handkerchiefs out of the dresser drawer that she always carried in her purse and laid it on top of the dress.

I then turned toward the dresser and watched myself in the mirror as I gingerly picked up the cigarette from the ashtray between my two fingers, put it just slightly between my lips, closed my eyes, and took a long, slow puff off it like I had seen the kids at school do.

Smoke immediately filled my lungs as I inhaled deeply and nearly strangled myself swallowing smoke and almost part of the cigarette. The room quickly filled with smoke. Where did it all come from? I thought as I tried to stifle my coughing so my stepmother wouldn't hear me and suspect anything. Panicking, I grabbed a newspaper and frantically fanned the air, trying to dissipate the smoke before she came back into the room.

I was a nervous wreck in those next few minutes. I just knew she would know. But when she came out of the bathroom, she didn't say anything, so I know she didn't have a clue what I had done. She would have loved the opportunity to jump all over me. I tried to hide my hands so she wouldn't see them shaking.

For days after that, I couldn't get the awful taste of cigarettes out of my mouth. I decided if this was what it was like to be cool, I wanted no part of it. That was my first and last attempt at smoking.

In elementary school, none of the kids cared what anybody wore. But in junior high and high school, it was important to look good. It was also important to have someone to pick on. And because of the way I dressed, I was a prime target.

In my freshman year, the girls in my classes soon noticed I was only wearing two dresses a week. They smiled and whispered among themselves.

One whispered loudly so that I could hear, "She's gonna wear that same dress tomorrow."

Another would say, "No way."

"You just watch."

And sure enough, I did. Once I tried making a feeble attempt at thwarting this game of theirs. Changing my clothes after school, I sneaked the black-and-white dress I had worn to school that day outside and rubbed the white collar on the pavement until it was smudged and dirty. I showed it to my stepmother and told her that somehow it got dirty at school and I would ask if I could wear another one the next day.

"How did you get it dirty? You only wore it two days," she said, eyeing me suspiciously.

I told her I rubbed up against something at school. She fussed at me but reluctantly let me wear another dress the next day. It was worth her being mad because for once, it really threw the kids off. I enjoyed that day immensely. But I didn't have the nerve to try that again, and I had to endure the jokes.

One evening, I was upstairs alone in our room. It had been a particularly harrowing day at school. High school was so hard. I usually bore the brunt of the jokes in my class, and that day was no different. And my stepmother started fussing at me as soon as I got home for something I hadn't even done, which happened often.

I was so miserable. I had tried so hard to please my stepmother and my teachers and make friends at school. But I had no friends because it was more fun to talk *about* me than *to* me. The teachers wouldn't talk to me at all. Sometimes they made me feel as if I was an outcast. At times, the way they looked at me, I felt embarrassed and dirty. And I was afraid to confide in any of them for fear they would tell my stepmother. Nobody dared to come over after school and visit us anyway because of her nasty attitude toward them.

I walked slowly to my brothers' closet—the same closet Mama had stood in years ago—and took one of their belts off the hanger, put it around my neck, and pulled as tightly as I could. But once I started struggling for air and my breathing was totally cut off, I couldn't go through with it, and I stopped.

Taking the belt from around my neck and with tears streaming down my face, I rested my head on the windowpane. Looking through my tears into the bright sunlight, I said, "Lord, I don't want to die. I just want somebody to love me."

I stood at the window, sobbing—my shoulders shaking with heaviness, my heart aching with loneliness. I stood there for a long time, even after the tears stopped, listening to the happy sounds of children playing on the sidewalk. After a while, I hung the belt back in the closet and sat down and did my homework.

My friend Janice lived almost directly across the street. Like us, there were six kids in her family and her mom and dad. She was the second oldest and had much younger brothers and sisters. With all the little ones running around, her house seemed to be in perpetual motion—lively, happy, chaotic in a good way.

The few times I was allowed to walk over to pick her up for school, I noticed the kitchen table was always filled with enormous amounts of food. I'd stand at the front door and stare in amazement.

"Janice, how come there's so much food on your table?"

"Because everybody wants something different, and we all eat at different times," she laughed as she examined a round loaf of bread that had gotten hard. "Mama's always cooking."

My mouth fell open. I didn't know what it was like to be able to eat all these different kinds of food.

Janice and I were in some of the same classes at school. I really liked her, and I called her my friend. But since I had to be home after school so quickly, we rarely got to walk home together or even really talk. Still, she kept trying.

One day, she decided to come over after school to visit me. When I answered her knock at the door, there she stood with a big grin on her face. I had never been allowed visitors before, so I didn't know how to handle this. I didn't want to tell her she couldn't come in, so with a slight smile, I nervously invited her into the living room.

After sitting there talking for a few minutes, my stepmother came to the door and said, "You better get up and dust this living room. You know your Daddy get off work at six. You sitting in here running your mouth. It better be done before he gets home. And you know you not allowed to sit in here anyway."

"Yes, ma'am," I replied.

She ignored Janice completely. If I could have crawled under the rug, I would have. Janice looked totally shocked and slowly shook her head in disbelief. She fidgeted around on the couch, wanting to leave but not knowing quite how. I immediately got up and started dusting. It was awkward trying to dust and talk to her at the same time.

A few minutes later, she whispered, "Gloria, I better leave."

"Okay. I'm sorry," I whispered back.

"It's okay, it's not your fault," she said, almost mouthing the words.

She never came in our house again.

Elementary school had been fairly easy, but I had difficulty getting good grades from junior high on through high school. I just couldn't seem to concentrate like I should.

9

My Favorite Subjects

Spelling and public speaking were the two subjects I enjoyed most in high school. I found it ironic that I would enjoy public speaking since I didn't get to express myself at home.

Our house was unusually quiet because of my stepmother's refusal to allow freedom of expression. We didn't feel free to talk unless we were upstairs out of earshot. Whenever she talked to us, it was usually in a threatening or yelling tone of voice or she was putting us down for something.

Mr. Phillips, my eleventh grade speech class teacher, was a small, animated man with horn-rimmed glasses who truly took pleasure in teaching. And he also took an active interest in each of his students and how well we all did. To him, it was important that we all learn to speak well.

We worked extra hard in his class as he coached us in preparing for the speech contest that was held at the school once every year. Each student picked a topic to speak about, preferably a famous person out of our history books or current events. And Mr. Phillips either approved it or suggested another topic. Upon his approval, we spent part of our class time researching and writing it. And after reviewing our topics with us individually, he then gave us tips on perfecting it.

It wasn't required, but he insisted we memorize our speech so that when we entered competition, we were fully prepared, confident, and needed no notes. To him, notes were too distracting in such a competition and also a sign of unpreparedness. He wanted us to have eye contact with our audience, and he also wanted us to win.

We spent hours researching and preparing our speeches. Voice inflections and proper gestures were all very important to Mr. Phillips. There were first-, second-, and third-place trophy winners and always many contestants. So competition was fierce among eleventh and twelfth grade students.

He encouraged us not to cheat ourselves by cramming at the last minute but to use every moment possible to push to the limit in studying and preparing for competition. We couldn't help but catch on to his excitement.

Before we knew it, the day of the competition arrived. The air in the auditorium was charged with electricity as proud and smiling parents arrived early in the morning for good seats. The grand event brought out the local newspapers, neighbors, spectators, and camera buffs. Students reported to homeroom classes for roll call and were then excused to the auditorium to either view the competition or take their places in it. Some were holding on to their notes like security blankets, hopeful they were not going to need them but too apprehensive to let go.

Taking my place with the rest of my class, I scanned the crowded auditorium and spotted my stepmother in the center section about six rows back near the aisle looking bored and distracted. I didn't think she'd come, but I was glad she showed up. I had worked so hard at my speech. And even if I didn't win, I wanted her to see that I wasn't the imbecile she kept saying I was.

Shortly after the nine-o'clock bell rang and everyone was finally seated, the noise and excitement subsided as our principal, Mr. Connors, arose from his seat and stood at the podium to extend a hearty welcome to all in attendance.

After his opening remarks, he turned to all of us in the competitors' seats and, with a flair and a sweeping wave of his hand over us, boomed out, "Let the competition begin."

A roar of applause resounded through the building as all the speakers stood up to be recognized, and then a hushed silence engulfed the auditorium as we sat back down; and the first contestant, notes in hand, made his way up to the podium.

As I sat listening to each one, I was glad I was going to be near the end. I thought I could get some mental tips from watching them on what to do and what not to do when my turn comes.

Each person received thunderous applause so that you couldn't tell which one the crowd favored. Each was so good that I began to worry whether I was going to be good, bad, or bomb out altogether.

Oh, God, I beseeched heaven. *Don't let me look at my stepmother. If she gives me one of her stony glares, I'm afraid I will lose my train of thought and have to resort to using my notes. And I've studied too hard and worked too long on this speech to let her affect me today. She doesn't care about me, but I know you do. Please help me do well.*

As my attention shifted back to the podium, I noticed the girl speaking in a booming voice suddenly left the platform and walked down off the stage out into the audience.

She confidently paraded down each aisle, lauding the praises of Thomas Edison, at times stopping to place her hands on her hips, wave her arms, or point at different people as if to personally include them in her presentation. She smiled broadly as she momentarily paused at the end of an aisle and pounded the wooden armrest. Even if you had never heard of Thomas Edison, she made you love him. She was not in my speech class, and I didn't know her, but what boldness and talent she exhibited. Who taught her how to parade around like that anyway? Who was her teacher?

I glanced around at the previous contestants who were now beginning to sink down in their seats, silently acknowledging defeat. Their mouths were open in utter amazement. No one had spoken this profoundly all morning. This girl was better than good.

Although some had walked around on stage during their speeches, no one had left the stage. No one had enthralled the audience like she had. We were mesmerized.

Finally, lowering her voice on the last sentence, she momentarily scanned the audience, walked back up to the stage, and then turned to face them. With aplomb, she gracefully held out her hands and said, "And that, my friends, is my version of a great man's life."

The crowd rose to its feet in a standing ovation. The applause was deafening.

We might as well stop right now, I thought.

She's won, hands down. I was next but felt glued to my seat. How can I follow that?

Wait a minute, didn't you just pray? I scolded myself. *Get your mind off her and get it on what you've worked and sweated to achieve.*

As the applause died down, my name was called.

All right, here we go, I told myself.

Squaring my shoulders and holding my head up, I walked up to the platform. As my eyes swept over the packed auditorium, I almost passed out. I never dreamed there would be that many people there. But I was determined to give my best performance. I knew my speech by heart but had brought my notes up just in case. Now I was determined not to use them.

Ignoring my trembling knees and avoiding my stepmother's gaze, I plunged into my speech. Using gestures I had practiced, I walked back and forth across the platform, elevating and lowering my voice at the appropriate times.

This feels good, I can do this, my subconscious mind was telling me. *As long as I don't look at my stepmother.*

My confidence grew with each sentence. On and on I went, drawing the audience in, making them feel as if they were in the hot sun picking cotton, riding on horseback with the plantation owner as he surveyed his crops and cotton fields, while, not far away, Harriet Tubman was leading three hundred runaway slaves, a few at a time, along the Underground Railroad to freedom.

Scanning the audience, I knew I had them. They didn't want to come back to reality. And on my last sentence, as the student before me had done, I spread my hands and smiling demurely, closing, "And that, my friends and neighbors, is my version of one of the great women in American history."

Returning to my seat smiling, I was still numb as the applause continued. Out of the corner of my eye, I could see Mr. Phillips clapping so profusely, he had almost knocked his glasses off.

I had no idea whether or not I had won a trophy, but I had won in a way none of the other kids could claim. For once and in my own way, I had defeated my stepmother. I had done something she would never have given me credit for doing. I felt ten feet tall.

The competition continued, and I crossed my fingers for each person as they gave it their best. They were all good. Finally, it was over, and the time had come for the panel of judges to announce the winners. Wistfully eyeing the three trophies on the platform, the students who had sunk down in defeat sat up expectantly to hopefully hear their name called.

Silence filled the room as one of the judges handed Mr. Connors the third-place trophy and the name of the winner. Smiling as he held up the trophy, Mr. Connors looked over at our section and hesitated, savoring the moment before he announced, "And the winner of the third-place trophy is Verlon Stokes."

It was pandemonium as Verlon jumped to his feet, shouting, "Yeah, yeah!"

He held his trophy high as flashbulbs clicked all around him. His mom and his brother ran from the audience and enveloped him in hugs. He was elated. After order was finally restored, it was time to announce the second-place winner.

Mr. Connors now holding the second-place trophy in the air, announced again, "And the winner of the second place trophy is Gloria Byrd."

Momentary silence. With big grins on their faces, my classmates all turned to me and loudly whispered, "Gloria, that's you!"

"What? That's me. You mean I won? I won?" I made my way up to the platform in a zombielike state, amid the cheers and popping flashbulbs.

I was in a complete state of shock. Hoping like all the others, I had still doubted that I would win any one of the three coveted prizes.

This must be a dream, I thought, shaking my head.

I don't even remember hearing Mr. Connors' congratulatory remarks.

As I left the platform, my classmates all gathered, hugging and congratulating me. My stepmother didn't move from her seat. Sitting back down, I was only vaguely aware of the first-place winner being announced, the student who had paraded down the aisles and enthralled her audience. I was glad she had won. No one deserved it more.

At the end of the program, amid all the hugs and tears and proudly clinging to my gleaming trophy, I expected my stepmother to come over to the section where I was and join in the celebration. But when I looked over to where she had been seated, she was now standing but had not moved from her spot. Finally, as people began to leave, I walked over to where she was.

Grabbing my arm, she said abruptly, "Come on, let's go."

As we walked home, her only comment about the event was that it lasted too long.

Spelling was another of my joys in school. I entered every spelling bee from fourth grade up through high school, each year's competition more difficult than the last. Spelling was much more fun than other schoolwork. Getting good grades in spelling and speech were my only encouragements.

Whenever there was a spelling bee scheduled, each student received a long list of words to study, which I immediately perused to see how difficult they were going to be. Each list contained a few really challenging words. I took my list home and studied it diligently.

Since Daddy worked long hours and was rarely home, I couldn't tell him what I was doing in school. And my stepmother wasn't interested in my ability to spell or speak. When I won a spelling bee, she would say "That's nice," and sometimes she would just say "Yeah?"

I brought home trophy after trophy for spelling and three for speech. She put one of each on the bookcase in the living room, and the others I had to keep upstairs in the closet because, as she put it, she didn't want to dust all those trophies.

The last spelling bee of the year came my senior year in high school. Spelling bees were also held in the school auditorium with all students and teachers in attendance, but not with nearly the fanfare accorded the speech contests. In fact, very few parents attended the spelling bees because they were so common and were held during regular school hours.

There were some really smart seniors in this spelling bee. But out of about thirty students, boys and girls, it finally got down to two of us, and I knew her to be a straight A student. We spelled correctly all the words on the official word list. And then with that list exhausted, they had to bring out a new list neither of us had seen before.

This was not the first time this had happened. It's what keeps a speller's skills honed, being able to spell new and unfamiliar words without practice. This was going to be the real test though. Still we battled, correctly spelling each word and nearly going through that list.

But finally getting to the last page of the list, it came my turn, and I missed the word and came in second place. In all my years of school, I had never lost a spelling bee. This was my first loss ever, and I was devastated. But I couldn't blame it on anything or anybody. The words were new to me, and I had done my best. Somebody had to win, and somebody had to lose. I lost. Still, it hurt.

I went home with my self-esteem shattered. Before I could even tell her about the spelling bee, Joe punctured through my depressed mood by yelling at me about putting a dirty fork in the drawer the night before.

"How could you put this fork away with all this egg on it? You didn't even wash it."

"I'm sorry. I didn't know I missed washing it. I'll wash it."

"I know you will."

When she finally stopped yelling at me, I told her I lost the spelling bee. I was right at the point of tears.

She said "well" as she nonchalantly turned away from me.

I thought she was through yelling at me, and so I turned to go upstairs.

"Don't you walk away from me when I'm talking to you!" she screamed.

"Oh, I'm sorry. I thought you were through," I replied.

I stood there waiting for a further onslaught, but when she still didn't say anything, I slowly began walking toward the stairs. And without warning, she came up behind me and kicked me in the seat of my pants so hard, I fell to the floor and almost passed out. The pain was so intense that for a few seconds, I lost focus and could not get up.

Then I began to crawl to the stairs as quickly as I could before she could kick me again with those rock-hard penny loafers she was wearing. I gripped the stair railing and covered my mouth so she would not hear me sobbing in pain and anguish as I half crawled and half stumbled up the stairs to my room. I threw myself on my bed and cried into my pillow.

10

Raid Beets

Winters were brutally cold where we lived, and produce was so expensive, nearly everyone in the neighborhood had a garden. Those who didn't were older people and those with no children. Sometimes parents gave up their gardens when their children grew up and left home.

If one family had more vegetables than they needed, they would give some to another family or trade one thing for another. There were also produce stands dotting the highways throughout the city. I felt it ironic that with all the food around us, we so often went to bed hungry.

Our garden seemed to me to be the size of a football field. There were so many gardens around ours, I wondered how each family knew where theirs started and ended. Although I don't remember the term being used, I guess they were what you would call community gardens because for our neighborhood, they were all on the same acreage of ground, one adjoining the other.

When summer came and the crops we had planted were ready to be picked, Joe got us up early every morning to walk the few blocks to the garden to work in the garden pulling weeds or picking whatever vegetables were ready. There was always so much to pick because everything grew in such abundance. We never had scrawny crops.

Sometimes Daddy traded some of our vegetables with other neighbors too. We had a fifteen-cubic-foot freezer that was capable of holding hundreds of pounds of meat and frozen vegetables. Sometimes Daddy went to the slaughterhouse and bought half a cow or a pig and had it dressed to put in the freezer. So there was always steaks and plenty of different kinds of meat in the freezer. And the closet in the living room that held the strap and the switches was where my stepmother stored most of the jars of food she canned.

One day, one of Daddy's friends came by the house and brought us a bushel basket of beautiful golden yellow bananas. Daddy told us we had to eat all of them in the next few days because they wouldn't last for more than a week. We were so excited because we never got fruit to eat. They tasted so good. And to be able to eat as many as we wanted was the best thing ever.

We came back from the garden with bushel baskets of beets, string beans, corn and potatoes, and a variety of other vegetables—whatever was ready and we were able to pick. Sometimes we made two to three trips a day to the garden. I looked forward to shucking the corn and stringing the string beans. They were usually easy and quick.

Returning from the garden, we first sat everything on the floor in the kitchen until we could organize and decide which basket to work on first. We put down sheets of paper in the utility room and sat the corn and string beans on the paper. We left the beets in the kitchen because we needed the rest of the utility room to work in. The beets had to be peeled and sliced to be canned, which probably took the longest time of all.

But on this particular day, we brought back so much that we couldn't get to the beets because Joe wanted us to shuck the corn first. And if we finished that, the string beans were next.

So to keep any bugs off the beets until the next day, she took a can of Raid and sprayed the whole box of beets thoroughly. We had seen her spray around vegetables and boxes before until we could prepare them but never directly on them, soaking them the way she did this box. I slowly shook my head and watched as the Raid bubbled up and seeped through each beet.

What is she doing? I thought. *Those beets are going to taste just like Raid next winter.*

When we peeled and washed them, I tried to wash the Raid off the ones I did, even though I knew it was hopeless.

Sure enough, when she opened the first jar of winter, they had a horrible taste of Raid. I already hated beets, and these were the worst. I was afraid we would all get deathly sick.

My stepmother ate a slice out of the first jar.

"They're not that bad, are they?" she said to us kids.

We had to say no because we knew she would get mad otherwise.

"I'll give your Daddy the ones that aren't so bad and you kids can eat the worst ones," she said.

There were so many jars of them. And each time she opened a jar to cook for dinner, it was a sickening experience to have to eat them.

11

Report Card Day

I was able to maintain a B average in elementary school. But in junior high, my grades started falling, and each year of school became increasingly more difficult for me.

By the time I reached high school, spelling and speech were the only classes I excelled in. My other grades were mostly in the C range—even gym, which should have been the easiest to get an A in. But I didn't want to take a shower in front of the other girls because I was too self-conscious and my back and legs were scarred most of the time from beatings. So my grade was lowered for not showering and sometimes for not being able to dress and play.

No matter how hard I studied, when it came time to take tests, I was a nervous wreck. I was definitely not a test taker. I would stare at the questions on the test and try desperately to dredge up in my mind everything that I had studied. But the tests were still difficult, and my mind would at times go completely blank.

Ever since the first semester in junior high when I got beaten for bringing home a straight C on my report card, I vowed that would be my last beating for a bad card, no matter what I had to do. So I tried to study more and concentrate harder in order to bring up my grades. But even though I gave it my all, the next semester, I got another beating for bringing home a C plus, which was just a tiny bit higher.

My stepmother said, "A C is just too low, and you know it is. I expect As and Bs, not a card like this. I know you can do better. You have to be fooling around in class. Go get the switch. I promised you a beating if you got a bad card, and I always keep my promises."

But the truth was, she only kept her promise when it came to punishment. And since I had tried my hardest and done my best, there was only one thing left for me to do. I just had to wait for the right moment.

School didn't seem as difficult for Donnie and Al, and their grades were always better than mine. But even though I didn't feel I was an A student, I knew I should be doing better than my grades were showing. I knew I was capable of getting a B. But it was becoming more difficult every day to concentrate. History and literature were especially difficult for me.

The worse things were at home, the more I struggled in school. My mind was blocked most of the time, and I was always thinking about the next beating at report card time.

I thought about my new plan all through the next semester as I kept trying to get better grades. About a week before report cards came due, I hung around my locker, which was just a few feet from my homeroom door at the end of my first period class one morning.

After the teacher had left the room and all the kids had left to go to their next class, with my heart pounding, I sneaked back into the room, hurried straight to the teacher's desk, opened the bottom desk drawer where I had seen her retrieve blank report cards from before, and quickly grabbed one from the stack.

I refused to even entertain the thought of what would happen to me if I was caught. And I was afraid to take more than one in case my stepmother were to find it later or a teacher would see it in my notebook. I slipped it inside one of my schoolbooks and held on to it tightly for the rest of the day, afraid to let that book out of my sight.

When I got home, I went up to my room, took out the card, and filled in all As and Bs on it and signed all my teachers' names in their proper places the way I had seen them signed on previous cards. The teachers themselves probably would have been able to tell right away that their signatures had been forged, but I knew my stepmother wouldn't know. They looked pretty impressive to me. I hid it on a shelf in the closet.

SMALL SPACE

When report card day came, I signed my stepmother's name to the new card and switched it with the fake card and then took the fake card home. She looked at it and said, "That's nice," signed it, and gave it back to me.

She never even looked at the signatures or commented that for the first time, I had gotten all As and Bs in every class. And she still wasn't impressed after all I had gone through to get that card. Of course, I should have been glad that I didn't get a beating—and I was—but this time, it was more than that. I realized that I could beg, borrow, or steal; and nothing would make a difference to her.

12

Summer at Aunt Tick's House

Aunt Tick was my stepmother's sister. They were as different as night and day, heaven and hell. My stepmother was mean and nasty; while Aunt Tick was the kindest, gentlest, sweetest woman I had ever known. How could two sisters be so different?

Summers at Aunt Tick and Uncle Sneed's house had to be as close to living in heaven as one could get without being there. When they occasionally visited us, they begged our parents to let us spend summers with them.

"Why don't you let these children come and spend the summer with us? They got a whole two months with nothing to do," Aunt Tick would ask Joe, and she said that every year.

And my stepmother's answer was always, "They don't need to go nowhere. They got chores to do."

"Hazel," Aunt Tick was relentless one time, "this house is so clean, you can eat off the floor. Besides, they're good kids. They won't be no trouble. Tell me what they got to do all summer besides chores. And it's only a two-hour drive. We'll come and pick them up and we'll bring them back."

"I'll have to talk to James about it."

We held our breath in anticipation because it wasn't very often that she and Daddy relented and let us go. Of course we were ecstatic when they did.

But we didn't get to stay the whole summer, just two to three weeks. But they were the best weeks of our whole year. We had told them a few times about some of the things that were happening to us at home. And they were very concerned, but without being able to take us permanently, they felt they had no power to interfere. And so they lavished all the love on us that they could the few times we went to see them.

Aunt Tick's kitchen was small but always bright and cheery. Her kitchen window looked out onto a patio full of potted plants. Her yard was covered with beautiful green grass and colorful plants growing everywhere. I liked to sit at the table while she cooked and look out that window.

Sometimes we just sat and talked about nothing in particular and drank lemonade. Other times, I'd tell her stories of some of the things that were going on at home. I could talk to Aunt Tick about anything. No subject was off-limits. I always wished I could stay with them instead of having to go back home.

As we talked, Aunt Tick kept saying, "Lord, Lord. I never would have thought a sister of mine could be so mean to God's children. Of all of us kids, none of us turned out like she did."

Then she began to relate to me stories of when she and my stepmother were children.

"Oh, those were good times," she laughed as she reminisced. "There were fourteen of us kids, and Hazel was the baby. We had so much fun together, climbing trees, girls as well as boys, playing down at the creek—just doing stuff that kids do. The girls did everything the boys did. I think that's why we had so much fun all the time. We didn't have much, but we were so close."

"But now, Hazel was Daddy's favorite 'cause she was the baby. He gave that girl everything in this world she wanted. And she couldn't do no wrong. We could all get in trouble but not her."

"Then, Aunt Tick, how come she turned out to be so mean?"

"I wish I knew. There just ain't no call for her to be treatin' you all like she do. She didn't get beat a day in her life. Something's wrong with her head."

During our stay, Uncle T, Aunt Tick's son-in-law, took us swimming. We rode bicycles, shot marbles, jumped rope, and just had a good old time.

I was twelve the first time we were allowed to visit them. Some days during those visits, we stayed at our cousin Polly's house. There were so many things I wanted to do, I was almost giddy with excitement. I didn't know what to try first.

I had been wanting to learn how to cook for the longest time but never got the chance at home. So on our second visit when I was fourteen, I begged Polly to let me make a cake the first day I was there.

"Sure you can make a cake," she said.

I was surprised she said yes. But I had to remember—she wasn't like my stepmother. Even though I wasn't exactly sure what I was doing and had never made a cake before, I wanted to try. After all, it couldn't be that hard.

I had the perfect cake in my mind, a three-layer chocolate with white frosting. I read the recipe carefully, got out all the ingredients, and meticulously measured each item. I poured it evenly into two round cake pans and baked it. The layers rose a little unevenly, but Polly said it looked all right. So I frosted it, which made it look even worse. And it was still uneven. But I was proud of it. And I was pleased that it tasted pretty good.

It was my first experience at baking. When I had ventured to ask my stepmother to teach me to cook certain dishes, she snapped at me and said, "All you'll do is burn the food."

I wouldn't burn it if I knew how to cook it, I thought.

During the day, we played on the porch while Polly was doing housework and cooking dinner and Uncle T was at work. When he came home, he took us all to the store and bought candy and toys for us. He must have taken us to the store nearly every day we were there. All I ever asked for were comic books. He bought me some with large animated cartoon figures on the covers.

I was more interested in drawing those big lifelike characters that loomed at me enticingly from the covers than I was in reading the stories. And though I never drew at home and hadn't even thought about it, here at Polly and Aunt Tick's house, my mind seemed to open up and reveal to me a whole wonderful world of things that I discovered I could do—things that I took great interest in.

I spent time playing with Donnie and Al and other kids on the street, but my favorite thing was sitting on the front porch drawing comic book covers. I could sit all by myself and spend hours drawing cartoon characters. I never tired of drawing. Each time we visited, Uncle T always made sure that I had plenty of comic books to draw.

Every time I finished a cover, I went to Polly or Aunt Tick for approval. They always made a big fuss over me telling me how talented I was. I didn't know if I was or not, but it felt good to hear it.

I found Dennis the Menace to be my biggest challenge and my favorite drawing. He was much more difficult to draw than the other figures I had done. On one particular cover, Dennis was standing poised in his coveralls, ready for mischief, with an impish grin on his chubby face, one foot slightly raised in front of the other as if ready to take off and explore the world, fists clenched, and arms raised slightly forward, ready to spring into action.

I drew and drew until finally he was perfect, except for his shoes. Cartoon shoes were always a challenge to draw. I labored over those shoes, determined to get them exactly right. After hours of drawing, erasing, and redrawing—perfection. Of all of my drawings, I considered this my absolute masterpiece. My heart swelled with pride as everybody voiced their approval and encouraged me to draw more.

Our visits to Flint always ended much too soon. What fun we had had. We gathered up all our treasures, still excited about all the fun things and explorations into which we had delved. We arrived home, ready and eager to share it all with Joe and Daddy.

When we arrived, Daddy wasn't home, so he didn't get to see my drawings. But I proudly presented all of them to my stepmother. I just knew she'd like them. But I hadn't counted on her response.

When I showed her Dennis the Menace, I told her what a challenge he had been but that I had completed him perfectly.

She didn't even look at him or any of my other pictures but said to me, "Yeah, throw that stuff in the trash. All it's gonna do is clutter up the house."

I was tempted to try and hide my pictures, but I was afraid she'd find them because we had no privacy at all. I looked at each of them one last time before I threw them away. I stared at Dennis the

Menace the longest, closed my eyes, and held him to my chest before letting him fall from my hand into the trash.

A piece of my heart went in the trash that day, along with all my other drawings. But Dennis the Menace was the most difficult to part with. I felt as if I had lost a dear friend. That was the last time they let us visit.

We also came home speaking perfect English.

"How come you speak good English when you in Flint, but you can't do it when you at home?" Joe asked one time.

Polly and Uncle T had taught us to say "get" instead of "git" and not to use the word *ain't*, so our language skills had greatly improved in that short span of time. We came home proud of the improvement in our speech. But she got on us so much about it that we purposely went back to talking the old way.

13

Stepping in the Mop Bucket

Weekdays were tough enough, but weekends were the scariest because we were home all day, subjected to our stepmother's ever-changing moods. At least during the week, going to school mercifully got us out of the house.

On Saturdays, we awoke early and talked quietly, listening for noise downstairs. We were not allowed to get up until Joe yelled up the stairs, "Glo, it's time to get up."

The tone of her voice when she called us told us what kind of mood she was going to be in for the day.

On one such Saturday, the early morning sunshine streamed through our window as we lay in bed, listening to the birds singing outside our window. It was already a beautiful spring day filled with happy outside noises. But there was something ominous in her voice that morning that made us feel that things were not going to go well that day.

We never knew what set her off on any particular day, so we always tried to be extra quiet and stay out of her way. But some days, no matter what we did, one of us couldn't seem to avoid getting into trouble.

"Watch out, you guys," I told Donnie and Al. "It sounds like she's in a bad mood this morning."

We quickly got dressed and went about quietly doing our chores. We seldom talked while we worked. In fact, we seldom talked at all without her permission, unless we were secluded upstairs in our bedroom.

Donnie's first job that morning was to mop the stairs from the upstairs hallway down to the bottom landing that led to the living room. He filled the mop bucket with soapy water and put it on the second from the bottom step, went and got the mop, and proceeded to mop the stairs from the top step down, soaking two or three stairs at a time and then wringing out the mop and wiping up the soap.

I had started cleaning the bathroom but had to stop and go downstairs to get more cleanser to finish cleaning the sink. Donnie was mopping the last few stairs as I walked down.

Just as I got to the bottom step where the bucket was sitting, I accidentally stepped right into it, tennis shoe and all. Water covered my shoe and sock up to my ankle.

It was such a freak accident; I don't even know how I did it. His eyes wide, Donnie looked alarmed.

"Glo, what are you doing?" he said quietly through gritted teeth.

He didn't want to get into trouble by maybe having the bucket in the wrong place.

"Oh no, I'm in trouble now," I said softly, more to myself than to him.

Joe was right around the corner in the living room, and she had heard me step in the bucket.

She came over and peeked around the stairs, took one look at the situation, and said "What the hell did you do?"

"I'm sorry, Mama. I accidentally stepped in the bucket. It was an accident. I'll clean up the water," I said.

She almost ran to the closet to get the black strap. I was terrified.

"Why can't you do anything right?" She came at me in a blind rage with the strap as I stood cringing on the bottom landing.

She grabbed me by the shoulder and yanked me off the landing into the living room and began beating me. I threw up my arms to shield myself as she struck me in the head, face, and back repeatedly.

I was wearing an orange-and-white blouse that day that was tucked into my jeans and a short slip underneath. She beat me until all but one of the six buttons on my blouse popped off and went flying. And then she beat the blouse completely off me. It ended up on the floor, and she stepped on it as she continued beating me. I was left with the slip-on, which now had bloodstains on it. I don't know how long she beat me, but it seemed like an eternity.

When she finally stopped, she yelled at me, "Go clean yourself up" as she went and put the strap away.

I picked up my blouse off the floor. Through my tears, I tried to find the buttons but couldn't. Bent over, clutching my blouse to my chest, I made my way upstairs, passing Donnie on the landing, who had been afraid to move up to now.

Crying and bleeding, I changed my wet shoe and sock and then examined my blouse that was also torn and stained with blood. Since the buttons were missing and the tears were such that it couldn't be mended, I threw it in the trash. I took my slip-on off and washed the blood out of it in the bathroom sink.

I used a wet washcloth to dab at some of the blood on my arms and legs, but the washcloth was too rough. It hurt so bad and my skin was so torn that the blood didn't even stop. I hung the washcloth back up and tried using small pieces of toilet paper. Some of the blood soaked into the toilet paper without pressing on my skin too much. I couldn't reach my back. I could only see how bad it was by looking in the mirror. It was so bloody, it scared me.

I hung my slip-on on the bedpost at the foot of my bed and then went to my closet to try and find another Saturday blouse, hoping that I wouldn't bleed through. I already had scars before this beating that were beginning to heal but hadn't healed completely. Now they had opened up again.

Sometimes the beatings I received were so close together that I couldn't tell which scars were from which beating. There was rarely a week that went by when one of us didn't get beaten and sometimes up to three and four times a week.

Many times my body was so scarred, I couldn't take a bath because I couldn't tolerate the soapy water on my open wounds. We were only allowed to take baths on Saturday night. But even then, I would sometimes go in the bathroom and pretend to take a bath, only to really be washing the parts of my body that were the least painful.

Some Saturday mornings, whenever the mood hit her, we had prayer meetings in the living room. She'd tell us, "We're gonna have a prayer meeting before you all go off to do your chores."

No matter what we were doing, when she said "Come on," we had to drop whatever we were doing and join her in the living room in a circle where we held hands as she called on each one of us to pray. I groped for the right words every time. I had such a hard time praying because I knew she was hanging on to my every word. And I couldn't pray for what I really wanted anyway, not in front of her.

When Al prayed, I thought that he was good. But Donnie, boy, Donnie could pray. I don't know how he was able to do it, but he could pray the most eloquent prayers. Then after we had all prayed, my stepmother ended the prayer. And as always, before we were sent off to do our chores, she critiqued each prayer. She always attacked me first.

"You know your Daddy been sick. Why didn't you pray for him?" she would say.

"Oh, I forgot," I'd say, as if I actually had.

I didn't pray for Daddy on purpose, knowing she would accuse me of giving special attention to him in my prayers. And then I knew the slings and arrows would come.

"Why can't you pray like Donnie? He prays for all the right things. You the oldest, but he got you beat by a mile. You need to listen to him and learn from him."

She didn't give me a chance to answer. She kept on.

"If anybody is sick, he prays for them. He prays for all the neighbors, and he prays for me. He really knows how to pray. Al, your prayer was okay."

It was clear she only slightly approved of Al's prayers, but she never criticized him. She praised Donnie on and on. All during the day, she would remember things I said in my prayer and question me about it, "Why didn't you pray about this? Why didn't you pray about that?" How could God be pleased with a prayer circle like that? It was a complete mockery of what prayer should really be like.

From about my junior high year through high school, there were times when my stepmother would call me upstairs into her bedroom and have me sit in the chair against the wall on Daddy's side of the bed. She'd sit on the same side on the bed facing me and take out a deck of cards. She held the deck in her hand facedown. She turned a card faceup and laid it on the bed. Then she would tell me what the card was showing her. It didn't matter which card it was. It was going to be bad news.

I sat there fascinated, wondering how she could just look at a card and tell me what was going to happen to me in the future and why it always had to be something bad. I anxiously waited for good news but never got any. She stared at each card thoughtfully, as if carefully measuring her words before she said them.

She told me I was going to marry a man who would be no good, would beat me, mistreat me, and cheat on me. Taking another card from the deck, she turned it over face up and laid it on the bed next to the first one. This card said I would have bad luck everywhere I went.

Laying the next card beside the previous one, she predicted that nothing good would ever happen to me, no matter what I put my hand to. I thought to myself that that was no different than what I was going through now. Another card said I would never amount to anything useful, and I wouldn't have any children. But if by chance I did have children, they would be unruly and would disrespect me.

Sitting quietly during these sessions, I didn't talk. I just listened, hoping at least one card would have a good prediction. She never elicited any comment from me but read continuously until she decided that was enough for the time being.

I didn't know why, but she never read cards on Donnie or Al. She kept on until she had read ten or fifteen cards—all bad news. How could she even think of all this stuff? She read cards on me periodically throughout the years. I soon stopped expecting anything positive from her readings.

My senior class took our cap-and-gown graduation pictures near the end of the school year. And when the proofs came in, the photographer brought them to the house for me to pick out the ones I wanted. He spread all the pictures out on the kitchen table. Washing dishes at the time, I dried my hands on a towel and walked over to see them. My, there were a lot of pictures.

"You ain't payin' for nothing," my stepmother snapped at me. "Get back over there and wash those dishes."

Embarrassed, I turned and went back to the sink without a word.

The photographer gave her a startled look and then stared at me as if he couldn't believe what he had just seen. He waited for a reaction from me. After all, they were my pictures, and I was entitled to see them and pick out the ones I wanted. But I wasn't stupid. I didn't dare look at him again.

"I like this one," my stepmother said, bringing the photographer's attention back to her.

Which one is she picking? I wondered. *I hope it's a decent one of* me.

I wanted to see them so badly. This was supposed to be part of the excitement of graduation.

"Wouldn't you like for your daughter to see them so she can pick out her favorite ones?" the photographer ventured.

"She ain't buying no pictures," she snapped. "Me and her Daddy are buying them. She gonna take what we pick or she don't get no pictures at all."

"What about the class ring? You do want to see the class rings, don't you? They're really beautiful this year."

"She ain't gettin' no class ring. I ain't paying that kind of money for a class ring. What is she gonna do with a class ring anyway? She don't need one. She better be glad she getting' a picture."

I wondered what the photographer guy was thinking. I'm sure he's never encountered this kind of situation before.

I had seen the rings at school, and he was right. They were beautiful this year. But there was no way I was going to be getting one. The only picture I got to see was the final one I picked up on picture day, the one she had chosen. Of course I didn't like it. I never did see what the other ones looked like. I was sure I would have liked one of them better than the one she chose. But like she said, I wasn't paying for them.

14

Working at Leo's

After graduating from high school, there weren't many jobs around for new graduates. But I had been asking my stepmother to let me take a job working at Leo's, a small family-owned restaurant that was only about three blocks past the high school we went to. To my surprise, she did.

Leo's had a counter, three booths, a few tables, and a jukebox. With a short and stocky build and a ready smile, Leo, the owner, had a big heart and knew everybody who came in. But he was really popular with the high school kids who poured in after school to listen to their favorite hits on the jukebox.

They loved his chili dogs and shakes. They were known as the best around. One of his thick shakes almost filled two glasses. He gave large helpings of food and, many times, free soda refills. Two people could eat off one order of his burgers and fries.

Sometimes he failed to charge full price when he knew some kid was struggling or didn't have much money. And at times, he would wave a teen off and not charge him anything. He was also known to be a good counselor as he sometimes sat and listened to different ones confide in him about their problems.

My shift started at six in the morning. In the summertime, I walked the three miles to work. In the wintertime, it was cold and dark, so Leo picked me up at home. He told my stepmother it was too dangerous for me to walk that far in the dark. He also let her know that he passed right by our street on his way to work. She didn't like the arrangement and told him that I could walk. She didn't like anybody being nice to me. But he finally convinced her to let him stop by and get me.

Leo let me try my hand at making various dishes. I soon learned how to make banana pudding and peach cobbler, and they became part of the regular dessert menu. We always sold out in no time.

I didn't make much money at Leo's, but it felt good to be trusted and to be a little independent. And it got me out of the house and away from my stepmother for a time. When I was at work, I was happy.

My stepmother didn't ease her stranglehold on my life, though, just because I now had a job. Now that I was working, she and Daddy felt that since I still lived at home, I should not only pay for rent but also for food and laundry. So by the time they took money from my check for all my living expenses, I only had five dollars left. And before the week was over, she had taken the rest of that. She called it "borrowing," but she never paid any of it back.

The only money I was able to hold on to that she didn't know about was the few tips I got. At Christmastime, though, I made good tips. And when I tried to keep that money to myself, she prodded me for it, saying that she knew I made good tips for the holidays. She didn't even believe me when I told her I hadn't made but two or three dollars each day, which I would give to her to appease her. I didn't mind paying my way at home, but I thought it was unfair that they took every penny I made.

There was no use trying to buy anything for myself because she questioned the need to spend money since I lived at home. She knew everything I had, so there was no way I could come up with anything new without her knowing about it. I couldn't hide anything from her, so the few dollars in tip money that I kept back, I still ended up giving to her.

After working at Leo's for approximately a year, Leo bought a larger facility in the downtown area, about ten miles farther from home, and asked me to go work for him there. I told him I knew my parents wouldn't let me go. They would say that it's too far.

Even though it would only be a short bus ride, my stepmother had always said that I was too stupid to go anywhere without getting lost. She said Donnie or Al would probably be able to do it, but not me, even though I was the oldest.

She didn't like or trust Leo. But he was a good boss and the only person who had ever treated me with respect. And he gave me more freedom at work to cook as I excelled at my job.

I could see the compassion in his eyes when I would tell him bits and pieces of my home situation. I never told him very much because I knew he couldn't help me anyway. He always listened quietly but rarely commented. Although he was able to help some of the kids who came to his restaurant with their problems, I knew my situation was beyond his help.

In the hopes that she might say yes, I told my stepmother that Leo was moving uptown soon and asked her if I could go to work for him at his new place. I held my breath as I waited for her response.

"No, absolutely not," she said. "You don't need to be going that far just to go to work."

If I couldn't go to work for Leo, I would be out of a job, and jobs were not that plentiful. I had enjoyed working, and I didn't want to quit to sit at home all day. What else could I do? If I didn't work, she would gripe about me being underfoot all day. I would be absolutely miserable being at home again. I couldn't understand why she wouldn't want me to work. But I didn't say any more about the move to her.

She didn't think anything I did or said was important. I was now nineteen years old and felt that the time had come where I had to find the courage to take the biggest step of my life. It would be my first real important adult decision, and I knew it was going to cost me. I just didn't know how dearly.

I realized my stepmother would never consider me grown-up and capable of making my own decisions, no matter what I did or how smart I proved to be. I would always be a nobody in her eyes.

Leo started moving into his new facility about two weeks later and had everything moved in a few days. He sold his little restaurant to a young couple who came right in and excitedly took over. The morning came when he was to have his grand opening. I secretly told Donnie and Al that I was going, but I didn't say anything to my stepmother.

I left home early, as usual, walking and not catching the bus until I was out of sight of the house so as not to draw suspicion. I took the bus that stopped in front of Leo's old place the rest of the way to the new place. I marveled at how easy it was to get there in spite of the negative picture my stepmother had painted about me.

I walked into Leo's new restaurant, overwhelmed at its enormity. It was absolutely huge compared to the previous place. Two waitresses besides myself from his old place were there. He had also hired several new people who were to start that day. They were beginning to come in one by one.

"Oh, Gloria, I'm sure glad to see you," Leo said excitedly. "I really need you today. I got all these new waitresses, and I'm going to need your help in training because none of them have much experience, and I hope to have a good turnout today."

Then he asked me, "How did you convince her to let you come?"

"She told me I couldn't come," I said. "But I left like I was going to your old place. She doesn't even know it's closed and that I'm here."

"That's not good. She's gonna be mad when you get home."

"I know, especially since she already told me I couldn't come."

I didn't know how long I dare worked that day, not knowing what was going to happen when I did get home. So I plunged into my work and tried to blot my stepmother's face from my mind. I kept telling myself I did the right thing, that it was time I grew up and took a stand for myself. But as the day wore on, my stomach began to knot in fear.

Four o'clock came and went, the time I usually got off work. She would surely figure out what I had done when I wasn't home by 4:30 p.m.

I had told Leo at 4:00 p.m. that I should be leaving. But we were still so busy, he was begging me to stay. The restaurant had been packed all day. As soon as one person or group of people left, another group walked in. And the dinner crowd was now beginning to show up.

By 5:30 p.m., I told him I just had to go. I knew I was in big trouble at home. He was too busy to take more than a minute to say goodbye.

"What are you going to do now? What if she tries to beat you?" he asked me.

"Oh, I know she will," I said. "I just don't know how bad. This is the first time I've ever disobeyed her like this. I don't know what's going to happen to me. I've tried to prepare myself for this, but I'm really scared."

"Maybe she'll realize you're grown-up now and she won't bother you."

"No. I know her too well. She will be furious with me. I'm sure she knows by now what I've done. She probably can't wait until I get home."

"Do you think you'll be able to come in tomorrow?" he asked, looking hopeful.

"I don't think so, Leo. I'm sure I won't."

I said a quick goodbye to everybody and left the restaurant, walked to the corner, and waited about ten minutes until the bus showed up. I sat by a window seat, looking out at the traffic, wondering how the day would end. I looked longingly at the restaurant until it was out of sight. I never saw Leo again.

I had been on the bus only a few minutes when, gazing out at traffic, I suddenly spotted Daddy driving slowly by in the opposite direction.

Oh no, I thought. *There's Daddy. He must have gotten off work, gone home, and Joe had sent him to find* me.

He was looking around, peering into other cars as he was driving and also trying to pay attention to traffic, which was getting heavy due to the hour. As his eyes searched the streets and then the bus, his gaze locked onto mine. And without any sign of recognition, he turned his car around and drove toward home. I was sick to the very pit of my stomach.

I felt so small sitting on that big bus.

Why can't I just get off this bus and walk away and nobody would ever find me? I pondered. *Where would I go? I don't know or care. I just want to disappear. I am so tired of being hated and beaten.*

With my hands folded in my lap, I stared down at the scars on my arms that had started to heal from the last beating I had received a few days ago. I couldn't even remember what the beating was for. It didn't matter anyway. One just simply followed the other.

It was after six o'clock when I walked into the house. They were both standing in the kitchen, waiting for me. Mama got me first.

"Didn't I tell you that you couldn't go with Leo? Why did you deliberately disobey me and go all the way out there without my permission?"

"Mama, I'm sorry. I didn't mean to disobey you. But you told me I couldn't go, and I didn't want to be without a job. I just wanted to keep working."

"I know what you doing," she said. "You having an affair with Leo."

"No, Mama. I just like my job, and I didn't want to have to quit."

"I never expected you to disobey us to this extent," Daddy said in a low, steady voice.

Daddy had never helped me before, but I was daring to believe that surely he would step in now. I was wrong.

"You know we can't let this go unpunished," she said. "This time, you went too far."

Finally, Daddy said those dreaded words to her: "Do you want to beat her or do you want me to?"

With a sinister eagerness in her voice that I knew spelled doom for me, she said, "I'll do it."

She told me, "Go on upstairs."

She went in the closet and got the dreaded black strap and followed me. Daddy went into the living room and sat in his recliner to watch TV. I was completely distraught and felt totally alone because not only was Daddy not going to help me; he was actually sanctioning this beating.

Once upstairs, she told me, "All right. Take that dress off."

I implored, "Mama, can I please explain why I went to Leo's?" I implored, shaking and terrified.

"Ain't nothing to explain. You blatantly disobeyed me. I told you not to go out there, and you went anyway."

I slowly took my dress off as I eyed the black strap in her hand.

"Lay across that bed," she said as I stripped to my slip-on.

She stood over me and began to beat me, hitting me with incredible force across my back, head, legs, and arms again and again, cutting into my skin, drawing blood with each powerful blow, seemingly releasing every ounce of hatred that was in her. With my dress off, the beating was much, much worse.

With each blow from the strap, my skin began to split open. Unable to stay down on the bed because of the violent blows, I jumped up several times, screaming in pain, begging her to please stop, only to be ordered back down.

"Get back down there!" she ordered.

As she kept bringing the strap down, the blood began coming through my slip, running down my arms and staining the blanket on the bed. I kept begging her to stop until my lips formed the words but no sound came out. It became even harder to get up off the bed. I felt as if my whole body was being ripped to shreds.

After more than half an hour, I knew I was going to pass out or die—I hoped this time, I would die so I wouldn't feel any more pain. When it was finally over, without a word, she stopped beating me and turned and went downstairs. I lay on the bed facedown, crying, now almost unable to move, weak, and gasping for breath.

Though my entire body felt as if it would never work again, I finally found enough strength to get up off the bed. Searing pain wracked me, and it seemed to take forever to change my slip and put my dress back on. I didn't even know why I was getting dressed again. It was already just about bedtime. But I didn't want to spark my stepmother's anger again by not showing my face downstairs. So I had to force myself to dress.

While I was trying to fasten my dress, Donnie came up, his eyes wide as he stared at the blood on my arms.

"Glo, Janice is outside in the front yard and she wants to see you," he said. "I don't know why she's out there."

"Donnie, I can't go down there like this. What does she want?"

"I don't know. But you may get in trouble again if you don't go down there."

I was in no shape to go downstairs, but I was afraid my stepmother might get mad again if I didn't go down. Although I had to pass by both of them watching TV, I don't remember leaving our room. I just found myself standing on the front porch.

Janice stared at me in wide-eyed disbelief. My arms and legs were bleeding. My face was tearstained. My back felt like it was on fire. I was unsteady on my feet and could barely stand up. I had to hold on to the banister to keep from falling down. She stepped back away from me as if getting any closer could cause me more pain.

"My God, Gloria. What did she do to you? She really beat you bad this time, didn't she?"

"Yeah," I breathed in between broken sobs.

It was difficult to talk to her because my breath was coming in short gasps. I thought I would stop breathing any second. My whole body was in shock.

"Are you going to be okay?" Janice asked, unable to take her eyes off me.

"I don't know. But I better get back in the house. I don't want her to get mad at me for being out here."

I had no idea why Janice came over, even though I briefly wondered if she was able to hear me screaming. No. She lived across the street. It was too far. I hadn't told anybody what happened that day, so she couldn't have known about that. I didn't ask her what she wanted, and she didn't tell me. Beyond that, I had no strength to think about it anymore.

Still having difficulty breathing, I somehow got back upstairs without them stopping me. They were both sitting in their recliners watching TV as if nothing had happened. I sat on the bed, looking at my arms and legs. With my two fingers, I gently took the skin in places on my arms and tried to close it up so it would stop bleeding. It hurt terribly to do it, and it didn't really work, although the bleeding slowed down in some spots.

After a while, I was able to carefully get in bed. I had to lay on my stomach throughout the night because it hurt too bad to lay on my back. I hardly slept at all.

Slowly opening my eyes, I realized it was Saturday and I had actually slept through the night. Marveling that I was still alive, I thought, *Why didn't I die last night? How much more pain can I take?*

My body ached even lying still. Not wanting to move, I lay still, listening for sounds downstairs.

"It's time to get up," came the familiar gruff call.

Barely able to pull myself out of bed and stiff with pain, I reminded myself, *It doesn't matter how badly you were beaten last night—you better get out of this bed or you'll get another one.*

I noticed my sheets had bloodstains in several places. I thought about washday. *What will she say when she sees all the dried blood?* I didn't care. I made up the bed anyway.

Since I had committed the ultimate crime of disobedience yesterday, I didn't know what to expect that morning. I wondered if today would be worse.

I got dressed as quickly as I could, although it was difficult to raise my arms or bend over. I didn't want to go downstairs because I didn't know if Joe was still mad. But I had no choice because I still had to go about my chores.

Holding on to the stair railing for support, I tiptoed quietly down the stairs to get the cleaning supplies. I held my breath as I rounded the corner into the living room, half expecting to encounter my stepmother with the strap still in her hand from the night before. I let out a sigh of relief when I didn't see her.

Daddy had already left for work, so whatever was going to happen that day, I thought I wouldn't even have him near for any kind of mental protection. And after last night, he probably wouldn't help me anyway. That day, she had free rein to do whatever she pleased.

I found her in the kitchen bending over the sink with the water running about to wash her hair. As soon as I passed her on my way to the utility room, she didn't even say good morning. She raised her head up out of the sink.

"You having an affair with Leo, ain't you?"

"No, ma'am, I'm not."

"Yeah you are. You're lying to me again. I told you 'bout lying to me. You thought you got beat last night. You wait 'til I get my head out of this sink. You gonna tell me the truth. You wouldn't have taken off like that for nothing, going way out there when I told you that you couldn't."

Turning back to the sink, she ignored me and proceeded to wash her hair. The fear from last night came rushing back in waves. I couldn't believe she was going to beat me again.

Picking up the broom and dustpan with shaking hands, I thought to myself, *I will never live through another beating like last night's. And as mad as she is this morning, I'm about to get another one.*

I went upstairs with the supplies and sat them down in the hallway. Donnie and Al were in our room starting to clean.

"Donnie, Al, I have to get out of here," I told them. "Joe is still mad, and she just told me she's gonna beat me again. I can't live through another beating like last night. She'll kill me this time."

"But, Glo, how can you leave? Where would you go?" Al said to me. "They would find you just like they always find Donnie."

"I'll take the bus to Flint," I said, trying to sound hopeful. "Polly gave me ten dollars last summer when they visited us. I've kept it hidden all this time. I'm glad I did because now I need it. Otherwise, I don't know what I would do. She said in case I ever needed to leave home, it would be enough to get me to their house for me to come and stay with them."

"Flint?" Donnie said incredulously. "You going all the way to Flint? None of us have ever been that far before."

Even Donnie in all his running away had never gotten more than a few blocks.

I told them I would miss them both, but I had to go. Since we had never been allowed to use the phone, I couldn't even sneak and call Polly to let her know I was coming. But they were my only hope.

"You guys tell her you didn't see me leave because I don't want you to get in trouble. Tell her you were cleaning and you don't know what happened to me. I don't want you to get a beating because of me."

We had had such a hard life together, and it hurt so much to leave them. I didn't even know when or if I would see them again. But that day had come to a life-or-death decision for me.

I rescued my ten dollars from its hiding place in the closet and hid it deep in the pocket of my jeans, took my white sweater off the hanger, laid it across my arm, and tiptoed downstairs. Cautiously entering the living room, I peered around the corner into the kitchen.

I could still see my stepmother bent over the sink washing her hair as I slipped back through the living room, out the back door, and silently closed the screen.

I was met by a happily chirping blue jay sitting on the banister of the porch seeming to beckon me, "Come on, let's play." It was only about nine in the morning, but already temperatures were in the mideighties, expected to reach the nineties by midday.

Running quickly around the side of the house, I stopped and put the sweater around me so nobody could see my arms. They were still raw and bloody. My back felt as if it was on fire, and I still hurt all over. Then glancing back to be sure she had not seen me, I ran between the houses out to the main road, observed only by Miss Bean's father, our neighbors who lived across the street from us and next door to Miss Flowers. In the summertime, Mr. Bean came out and sat on his front porch early every morning with his cup of coffee and his newspaper and watched the people pass by.

Everybody in the neighborhood always said "Mr. Bean sees everything." No matter what went on, he was sure to know something about it. But I hoped he wouldn't tell his daughter—at least, not until I got away. I didn't want her running over to our house to find out what was going on.

Mr. Bean's gaze followed me down the street. I didn't know if Janice had had a chance to talk to him about last night. But somehow, I sensed he knew I was running away.

Approaching the bus stop, I stopped running to catch my breath. I craned my neck in the hopes of spotting the bus before anyone spotted me. I didn't know who would come looking for me since Daddy had already left for work. But I was still paranoid that I wouldn't get away.

It was getting really hot now, and the sweater I had around me, although thin, was beginning to stick to blood spots on my skin and become very uncomfortable. But I didn't take it off because I didn't want to draw attention to myself. I caught the local bus to the second stop where the Flint bus, hopefully, would soon arrive. I won't be able to relax until I'm on that second bus.

Alighting from the first bus, I tried to blend into the shadow of Kay's Jewelry Store while I waited for the bus to Flint. There were about ten people standing around waiting on various busses. Suddenly, I looked up and spotted a patrol car slowly pulling up to the curb right at the bus stop. My heart pounded in my chest. I felt like a trapped animal.

How far could I run if I had to? What would I do if they tried to make me go back home? I thought, fearing for my life.

I held my breath as the two policemen eyed me suspiciously. They sat there in their car for a few minutes smiling and talking to each other, occasionally looking at me, and then drove off.

Thank God, I sighed. *That was close.*

Finally, the bus going to Flint arrived. Thankful for my precious bus fare, I took a seat in the back next to the window so I could look out, still fearing the worst. Eventually, we were out of the city, and I was able to sit back and close my eyes for a short while.

Two hours later, we arrived in Flint. I was glad to be far from home, but I was missing Donnie and Al already.

All of a sudden, a new fear rose up in me. What if Aunt Tick really doesn't want me to come or they don't have room for me? After all, I hadn't had a chance to call her or Polly, so they'll be totally surprised.

I tried to shove those negative thoughts in the back of my mind as I caught a cab from the bus station to their house. Soon, I recognized the familiar street and began to get a little excited.

As the cab pulled up to the front of the house, the door opened, and Aunt Tick walked out with a puzzled frown on her.

"Lord, have mercy. What you doing here, baby? What happened to you?" she asked.

Before I could answer, her ample arms enfolded me in a tight, loving embrace, which made me wince in pain. Uncle Sneed came out and paid the cab driver.

Eyeing me with a big smile on his face, he held out his arms and said, "I wondered if you'd ever come."

"I was hoping you wouldn't be mad at me for coming without calling you first," I responded.

"Now, Gloria," Aunt Tick said to me, "you know you're welcome here anytime. You don't need to call us. We're always here for all you kids. Don't you ever forget that."

We walked in the house together as I explained what happened and why I was there. I took off my sweater, and they looked at the welts and dried blood on my arms.

"I wore my sweater because my arms are so marked up. My back is worse."

Aunt Tick put her hand over her mouth and shook her head.

"I can't believe this. I just can't believe it," she kept saying. "This is terrible. Hazel has gone over the line this time."

They were both furious.

"Please don't call her, Aunt Tick. I don't want her to know where I am. I'm too afraid to go back home."

"Don't you worry, honey. You don't ever have to go back there if you don't want to," Uncle Sneed said as he got me a cold soda pop from the refrigerator.

"Have you had anything to eat?" Without waiting for me to answer, Aunt Tick started bustling around the kitchen making me a sandwich.

I suddenly realized I hadn't eaten all day and was hungry.

"I hadn't had a chance to eat yet," I told her.

I didn't know ham and cheese could taste so good. Sitting at the table with me drinking soda, they listened as I recounted in detail the events that led up to the beating the night before.

"I don't believe I'm hearing this. I'm gonna call Hazel. I've got to call her."

"Please don't call her, Aunt Tick."

"Listen, you don't have to be afraid of her no more. She can't hurt you here. And you don't have to go home until and unless you want to. So you just make yourself at home, you hear me?" Aunt Tick said, her voice was soft and soothing but slightly trembling.

"Yes, ma'am," I said, with uncertainty in my voice.

Aunt Tick left Uncle Sneed and me and went in the living room to call my stepmother. Uncle Sneed tried to keep me occupied by telling me how glad he was that I had come and taking me out and showing me his flower garden.

I had never heard Aunt Tick's voice so loud and angry. I could hear her even out in the garden. I wondered what lies my stepmother was telling her about me.

I had such a restless night that night that the next day, Aunt Tick took me to the hospital to be examined by a doctor. After a brief examination, the doctor wrote a few notes on a chart. Then with a solemn face, he turned to me and said, "Who did this to you?"

How could I tell him the truth? I was no longer at home, but I was still deathly afraid of my stepmother.

"I can't tell you," I found myself saying.

"It's okay," he said. "You don't have to be afraid. You can tell me."

That was the same thing Aunt Tick had said, but I still wasn't confident. They didn't know my stepmother. I felt like no matter where I went, she would somehow find me and I would pay for leaving home.

The doctor gently but firmly kept pressing me with questions until I told him, "My stepmother beat me."

I added, "I don't want her to get into trouble," but I was more afraid Daddy would get into trouble for letting her beat me. Even though Daddy had never come to my aid, I was still trying to protect him.

"We're going to fix you up," the doctor said as he ignored my comment, faking a smile. "You're going to be as good as new. I just want you to stay in the hospital for a few days so you can heal up and you don't get infection in those wounds."

While in the hospital, the nurses cleaned some of the open sores on my body and applied various sorts of creams and antiseptics to other parts. I dreaded the daily treatments. At times they hurt as bad as the beating itself.

As I lay there trying to take my mind off the pain, I wondered what would have happened if I had not run away that morning and stayed home and subjected myself to another beating, which I surely would have gotten. I know I would be dead today.

After a week's stay in the hospital, I went back to Aunt Tick's house for another week of recuperation and then moved in with Polly and Uncle T. I was still scarred pretty badly, but I was slowly beginning to heal. I had never gone this long without a beating, and nobody had yelled at me since I got here. It was wonderful.

I didn't want to be a burden to Polly, so after a week at her house, I went job hunting and obtained a job as a cashier in a grocery store. It turned out to be a very satisfying job, which I enjoyed very much.

After a couple of months working there, I rented a room from Miss Smith, one of Aunt Tick's sweet elderly friends who rented three of the bedrooms of her house out to supplement her income.

Every day after work, I changed my clothes, as I was so used to doing, and sat outside on the porch with Miss Smith's daughters who came almost daily to visit her; or I would go up to my room and sit in the chair by the window, staring out into space, my mind far away.

How is Donnie and Al doing? I thought. *I hope they didn't get beaten for not telling Joe I had slipped out. How many beatings have they had since I left? Why has she not called to talk to me? She knows where I am. Is she still mad after all these months? Is Daddy still mad at me too?*

I was more concerned that he was mad at me than I was with her. I didn't know if I was lonesome or bored, but I began to want more than a job and an evening alone in my room.

There has to be something out there for me, I thought, squinting my eyes hard out the window as if I somehow might be able to see my future if I looked far enough out.

And after daily mulling over in my mind all my options, I finally decided to join the army. But now a new problem arose. Since I was still under twenty-one, I needed the written permission from both my parents.

By now, six months had passed since I had left home. I had started calling occasionally, just to let them know I was okay. I didn't even know if they cared. My calls had been met with coolness on the other end of the phone. In spite of that, I wondered if by now I would be accepted back home. I had no intentions of going back to stay, but since I needed their signatures to join the service, I had to risk going home.

I chose a Saturday where I knew I wouldn't have to work. I called ahead to let them know I was coming so that my arrival wouldn't be a complete surprise. I didn't know how long I was going to stay. It would depend on how they treated me.

I told Aunt Tick about my decision, and she just told me to be careful when I went home. I think she was afraid of what my stepmother might do upon my return. I was more afraid than she was.

On impulse and almost as a peace offering, I decided to buy a watermelon from a street vender who was set up right near Leo's old restaurant. I knew I had to carry it a good ways after I got off the bus, but it would be worth it if they welcomed me back.

I picked out a pretty green one that looked ripe and wasn't too heavy. People driving down the street stared at me. I smiled slightly and averted my eyes, thinking I must look really ridiculous carrying a watermelon. I could read their minds. They would be wondering out loud, "Why is that woman walking down the street carrying a watermelon?" But they had no idea of the circumstances.

The closer I got to home, the heavier the watermelon got. I was only too glad to get in the house and put it down on the floor. Both my parents were sitting at the kitchen table, drinking coffee like they always did on Saturday morning when Daddy didn't have to work. I was glad he was there. They didn't even look up when I walked in.

"Hi, Mama and Daddy."

"Hi," they said.

After six months, that's all I got from them.

"I bought you a watermelon."

"That's nice."

I lightly hugged each one of them; but neither looked at me, returned the hug, or responded in any way. They sat stiffly, looking out the window.

This is not going good, I thought. *Now what do I do?*

I felt very awkward, not knowing what to say or how to act. I picked up the watermelon and put it in the sink.

Donnie and Al came in the kitchen and said hi to me. I could see the excitement in their smiles, but they didn't hug me. It was sure good to see them, but I couldn't act mushy just yet. I had to wait until we could get upstairs. I had worried a lot about them, thinking my stepmother might take her anger for me out on them. As soon as we had a chance, we escaped upstairs. We hugged and hugged. How I had missed them.

They told me how furious Joe was when she discovered that I had sneaked out and that she had called the police and told them I had run away for no reason. They asked her how old I was. When she said I was seventeen, they told her that I was now an adult and they couldn't make me come back home. Of course she didn't tell them she beat me.

Then I remembered the two policemen at the bus stop the day I left. They must have been looking for me. Now it all added up. She had even gotten mad at Donnie and Al for not telling her I left, but at least she didn't beat them that time.

I had been home for one hour when she brought up the incident of my running away. She wanted to know why I had run away that morning when there was no call to do so. I told her that I was afraid I would get another beating, so I had left.

Suddenly, that old fear that had been gone for six months returned. But in my heart, I had vowed I would never let her hit me again. If she had, I wouldn't have hit her back. I would have just left. Even with all she had done to me, I would not have retaliated.

I didn't tell her that I had spent a week in the hospital. Since she put me there, I thought why should she care anyway? She muttered something to herself and then dropped the subject, probably because Daddy was home.

Later on, when I asked them about signing the papers, Joe said she was not signing any papers, that the army was for men and not women, and that I had no business being there. She had said that same thing when I had tried to talk her into letting me take driver's education in high school. She felt that women didn't need to know how to drive and that teaching them was a waste of time and money. And even though the classes were free, she still didn't let me take it.

"Why on earth would you want to join the army?" Daddy asked me.

I didn't know what to answer, so I said I thought the experience would be good for me. Secretly, I was just wanting to get far, far away from my stepmother, just as my older brothers had done. And this was the only way I knew how to do it.

Finally, after a discussion between themselves, neither wanting to relent, Daddy told her, "I guess we might as well sign these papers because she'll find a way to go if she wants to go bad enough."

They both signed.

I stayed until the next morning, more for Donnie and Al's sake than for any other reason.

When I got back to Flint, I turned in my service application at the induction center and a few weeks later was on my way to Fort McClellan, Alabama, for basic training.

15

Boot Camp

Excitement ran high on the army base as young women gathered from different states to begin the grueling process that would separate the men from the boys, so to speak, and eventually turn us all into disciplined soldiers. But that excitement soon fizzled as I, along with thirty-four other young women, were ushered into what would be our new living quarters for the next eight weeks.

This was nothing like the colorful snapshots that we had seen in the bright brochures that came in the mail or the large poster boards that stared at you invitingly from the bulletin boards on the school walls, luring us into a fabulous career in Uncle Sam's Army.

The part that had stuck in my mind the most were the serene, peaceful views of the ocean, glamorous hotels in the background, the elegantly swaying tall palm trees and the phrase that dominated every poster, "Travel and see the world. Join the Army." How naive we all were.

There was certainly nothing glamorous about this place. We all felt trapped among dingy gray-white prison walls. The huge room we were now going to live in was called a bay. We felt dwarfed by the drab high walls. A small window high over each person's bed had no curtains. You couldn't see out of it anyway, unless you stood up on your cot on your tiptoes. Thirty-five army cots side by side were covered with the ugliest green army blankets I had ever seen. Separating each cot from the other was a small, dark brown nightstand for each person.

We all picked out a bed and reluctantly began to unpack the few belongings we were allowed to bring. I sat on my bed and tried to imagine what the next eight weeks would be like. Some sat, staring into space. Some cried. Some wrote home. For a while, few talked.

There were five companies on our base, Companies A, B, C, D and E. Each company had bays and each bay had a person in charge. Our bay was in Company D.

Our first week was filled with basic induction preparation, picking up necessary supplies, and filling out hundreds of forms. It was almost funny when we went to the warehouse-like location to pick up our clothing. The sergeant in charge of handing out our uniforms looked us up and down and, without a word, handed out to each one a prefolded set of uniforms, dress hat, work clothes, and shoes that he thought would fit each of us.

Back in our bay, unfolding and sorting our new outfits, we were quite surprised that he had actually guessed our sizes almost perfectly. These rough dark work clothes were still something we'd have to get used to though.

Each bay had a sergeant assigned to oversee us, take us to our classes, teach us how to drill, give us our work assignments, and basically get us through basic training. We learned survival techniques, how to read maps, gas mask training, and various other informative classes. It was interesting but tough.

A week into our training, my captain called me into her office. All the girls wanted to know what I had done. I didn't think I had been there long enough to get into any trouble.

After a short greeting, my captain informed me she was making me bay sergeant, which meant being in charge of my thirty-four companions. And I, in turn, would report to my sergeant, who had other duties. I was too shocked to be flattered. How could I possibly take on this kind of responsibility when my stepmother didn't even think I could catch the bus?

My captain also informed me that my new assignment included making sure all the girls kept doctor and dental appointments, showed up to their work assignments on time, attended all the drills, and, most of all, obeyed the rules and stayed out of trouble.

I had no idea how or why she chose me since I hadn't had a chance to prove my abilities. But I planned to do my best to show her I was capable, if indeed I was.

Wait until I write home about this, I thought.

I can almost hear my stepmother saying "well."

All the girls respected and supported me, and we became like a big family. I made sure that they were all on time for everything and nobody missed drills or classes.

When one person wasn't in the barracks at bed check time, we put blankets in the bed to make it appear she was there. It didn't happen very often because it was a serious offense if anyone was caught out after ten-o'clock bed check. But we protected one another.

Just about every offense was considered serious because they were trying to teach us discipline. And since I was in charge, I was going to do everything I could to keep everybody in line because I didn't want to get in trouble either. However, I had my work cut out for me with a few of the girls who were not used to taking orders or living under such strict conditions.

They would miss doctor or dental appointments. If they didn't show up for drill, I had to go and get them. Sometimes they came in late on Friday night or were just defiant toward authority.

My biggest challenge was Sandy and Lucy who were in an illicit relationship. They spent as much time together as they could, sometimes completely oblivious to the rest of us. Many nights after bed check, Lucy would tiptoe out of her bed and slip into Sandy's bed. We would find them asleep together in the morning.

I was constantly chewing them out, trying to make them aware of the dangers of what they were doing. Even though they apologized, they kept getting in each other's bed. Sometimes I caught them holding hands in the mess hall. Other women who knew what was going on looked at them and smiled. Since we were all like family, nobody squealed on anybody.

But I had to tell them, "You girls know that we will all protect you, but if the sergeant or the captain catches you doing anything at all, you could be kicked out of the army."

"It's not Lucy's fault," Sandy said, accepting the blame. "I shouldn't let her get in bed with me. I know it's dangerous. We don't want you to get in trouble because of us."

"But you're both my friends," I pleaded, "and I don't want either of you to get in trouble. But you've got to cool it because I think the captain is already suspicious. Don't spend so much time alone."

Unfortunately, a few nights later, Lucy again crept into Sandy's bed. At midnight, I was awakened by a bright flashlight in my face and the captain's loud voice calling me.

"Gloria, wake up. Didn't I tell you to watch these women? You see what you've let happen?"

Still half asleep, I jumped up, dazed. Somebody else jumped up and turned on the lights. Looking over at Sandy's bed, she and Lucy were both sitting up now but obviously distressed over being caught together.

"I'm sorry, Captain. I didn't mean for this to happen."

"Then you should have done something about it. I want you in my office first thing in the morning."

Shifting her angry gaze to Sandy and Lucy, she retorted, "You two are in big trouble."

With that, she turned on her heels and walked out. We all took turns hugging Sandy and Lucy, trying our best to comfort them as they cried and repeatedly apologized to us. None of us slept much the rest of the night knowing what was going to happen in the morning.

The next morning when I reported to the captain's office, she chewed me out, which I didn't mind too much. But what hurt me the most was that at the same time, Sandy and Lucy were being discharged from the Army. I cried again when I got the news. We were going to miss them.

Soon after becoming bay sergeant, my captain bestowed on me the coveted honor of being drill instructor for my bay. Even though we had been drilling every day, I didn't know the first thing about being a drill sergeant. That meant learning how to march in drills and parades, honoring officers, and just marching because we were in the military and that's what you did.

Each company drilled every day, marching for miles in the hot Alabama sun. Sometimes companies went out at different times of the day, sometimes all at once. Temperatures could reach as high as one hundred degrees. But we drilled anyway.

Our assignments for the week were posted on a large bulletin board in the hallway so we could see at a glance what duties and classes we were assigned to each day. And drilling in the heat was fitted into every day's schedule. After all, that's why we were there.

The first day I took my team out to drill on my own, I was hoping I wouldn't make any mistakes. That day, we and a couple other companies practiced on a huge football-sized field. Each company was spread out far enough to train so as not to march into the others.

As I marched my group up and down our portion of the field, at one point, we were nearing an eight-foot brick wall. I realized I had to do something to keep them from marching into it. But I couldn't for the life of me remember the command for an about-face, so I yelled, "Stop, stop. Halt."

Well, they are only supposed to stop on the proper command. So they all just kept marching until they reached the wall and marched right into it. When they hit the wall, they just stood there marking time. Then we all fell up against the wall and broke out in peals of laughter. As some fell on the ground in hysterics, I frantically looked around to see if any of the other companies had seen us. I was glad nobody appeared to notice. It was times like that that we actually had fun drilling.

It wasn't long before we all had blisters on our feet from all the marching. Sometimes the blisters were so bad, we had to march on the sides of our shoes, which was not easy. During parades for top brass, all the companies were required to march without exception.

We stood for so long at parade rest during summertime ceremonies that some of the women fainted from the intense heat. We were not allowed to break rank to assist them, so they lay on the ground until they revived. I never fainted, but people went down all around me.

At the end of each ceremony, we marched off the field, stepping over women who were still passed out on the ground, trying not to trip on them, and still having to march in sync. It seemed cruel to do that, but that's how it was. But we all shaped up and made it through boot camp.

After boot camp, we were given three choices for where we wanted to serve the remainder of our tour of duty. I had heard so much about sunny California—that's where I wanted to go. Since I had never been anywhere anyway, I didn't care about anyplace else. If I couldn't have California, it didn't much matter where I went.

There were squeals of delight as several of the women got their first choices. Some groaned at getting their second choices. Some cried at getting their third choices because they were leaving boyfriends behind or it placed them farther away from home.

Since we had gotten so close, separating was very painful because we knew that we would probably never see one another again. There were lots of tears and hugs on graduation day from boot camp. But we would be taking with us good memories and cherished friendships.

16

Tour of Duty–Sunny California

My assignment turned out to be Presidio, San Francisco, my first choice. The base was even larger than the one I had just left. The bays were brighter and in much better condition than those at boot camp. Since we had learned the basics, it became easy to adjust to our new surroundings. We fell into our job duties quickly and much more enjoyably.

Every morning at 5:00 a.m., we assembled in the courtyard for roll call, morning inspection, and orders. On payday, for who knows what reason, roll call was at 4:00 a.m. One payday morning, I overslept and awoke startled by the words "fall out" over the intercom.

Oh no. How could I have overslept? I chastised myself.

Like lightning, I scrambled out of bed, threw my uniform on as fast as I could, and dashed downstairs outside to fall in line with the others for roll call. But the captain had already called out my name. She noticed me ease into the line.

After roll call was over, addressing me in crisp, severe tones, she said, "Private Byrd, report to my office."

I followed her to her office where, after handing me my paycheck, she chewed me out for oversleeping.

"What did you do last night that kept you from getting up this morning?"

"I didn't go out last night, ma'am. I was here in the barracks. I don't know what happened, but it won't happen again."

"I hope not, for your sake. But just so you remember, I want you to go change into your work clothes and come back here."

I had no idea what she was going to make me do, but I hurriedly changed and ran back to her office. She was standing in her doorway with a broom in her hand.

"I want you to go sweep the dirt out of the ditch outside," she said.

As I looked at her, puzzled, she further said, "The ditch right out here in front of my office next to the mess hall. Sweep the dirt out."

The ditch was located several feet in front of her office window and a few feet from the mess hall. I thought it was a ridiculous punishment, just because I overslept once. I hadn't missed the entire roll call, and I was only late by minutes.

Well, I thought I had the whole day to do it. But she surprised me as I turned to leave by telling me, "I want you to sweep now during breakfast."

When I went out to the ditch, women from the various companies were on their way to the mess hall. Some had begun to gather in small groups outside, waiting for friends. Several of the men also came over daily from the various offices and surrounding bases for breakfast.

So this is what she had in mind for me, public humiliation, I thought wryly. *Why didn't she just announce it over the loudspeaker, "Gloria overslept"?*

I was not allowed to talk to anyone or my punishment would double, whatever that meant. I could see myself scrubbing the barracks with a toothbrush.

When I reached the ditch, I looked down into it, and I almost laughed. A ditch full of dirt. How do you sweep dirt out of a ditch when it's nothing but dirt to begin with? This is crazy. It was about five feet deep, an inch deeper than I was tall, and spanned the length of the building where we were housed. I glanced over toward the captain's window where she was sitting watching me, and she pointed to the spot she wanted me to sweep.

This is so ridiculous, I thought, jumping down into the ditch and fighting the urge to sing. *She'll think I'm being funny, so I better cool it. I probably look as foolish as I felt.*

As I lifted my broom and began to sweep the dirt up and out of the ditch, it flew up into the air in slow motion and billowed right back down on my head and in my face. I was soon covered from head to toe in dust and dirt. At times I had to close my eyes and mouth to keep the sand and debris out. Now it's not funny.

As people passed by, they laughed and jeered at me and asked me what in the world I was doing or why was I sweeping dirt out of a ditch. Some of them had seen these types of ridiculous punishments before, and a few had even undergone the exact same punishment themselves. But when it's not you that's being punished, it's easy to laugh at somebody else's misfortune.

Every time I checked the captain's window, she was still sitting there with her hand on her chin, staring out at me, obviously enjoying the scene. I wanted to throw dirt on some of those who were laughing, but I had to ignore them.

After about an hour and a half, breakfast was over, and the crowd had diminished. The captain called out of her window to me that I could stop now—after total humiliation. I had missed breakfast, but I didn't care. I certainly wasn't hungry then. I just wanted to get out of that ditch and take a shower. My arms and hands ached, and I was totally exhausted. But believe me, that was my first and last time to oversleep.

17

A Bad Marriage

Not long after arriving in California, I met Louis who had five children and had recently lost his wife to cancer. The first time I saw them, they were ragged and dirty, and my heart went out to them. They didn't even look as if they had a mother. I thought about my own painful past. His oldest was sixteen and in a mental institution, having gone into deep depression after his mother's death.

I immediately befriended his children who took to me right away. Louis and I dated off and on, but my army duties were so demanding that I didn't have much time for him or them. But we continued to date periodically. And near the end of my term of service, we were married.

I soon discovered I didn't really know much about him. I mistook his earlier attention and kindness for genuine love. And I had slipped into this relationship completely unaware of its pitfalls.

Louis drank and gambled to excess and rarely stayed home. When he did come home to eat dinner, in spite of my protests, he ate with his hat on and left as soon as he was finished eating, returning home in the early morning hours. Sometimes he would be gone for two or three days at a time and would return in the middle of the night, offering no excuse.

When I tried to talk to him about his carousing and drinking, our lack of communication with each other, his neglect of his children, and the problems our marriage was experiencing—he'd say, "If there's a problem, you have the problem. I don't." And to avoid any further confrontations, he'd leave the house as quickly as possible.

I put all my efforts into being a good mother to his remaining four sons who ranged from ages six to fourteen years. I encouraged them to talk about their mother whenever they wished. I was not going to put them through what I had gone through.

They constantly asked me, "Gloria, why doesn't Daddy take us fishing? Why doesn't he do stuff with us?"

I scrambled for answers that wouldn't make their Daddy look bad, but all my reasons were soon exhausted.

Not long after we were married, I became pregnant. Louis had gambled in the past, but now he gambled more often and was gone for longer periods of time. Women started calling the house, asking for him. When I confronted him about it, he claimed he didn't know who they were. But I knew he was cheating on me.

He began telling me how fat and ugly I was. I was pregnant, for gosh sakes. He told me not to go out of the house because of the way I looked. Naturally, I became very depressed. And as I got bigger, I began to eat, even when I wasn't hungry.

My doctor warned me I'd better cut down on my eating because I would definitely be facing a difficult delivery if I didn't. He put me on a no-fat, low-sodium diet and strongly advised me to watch my weight. I took the bland diet home and asked Louis if he would help me stick to it. He told me it was up to me, that he didn't care whether I stuck to it or not. If I couldn't keep my weight down, he told me not to expect him to help me.

In spite of his comments, I really tried to follow the doctor's orders. I did not want to gain any more weight. But food with no salt was completely tasteless. And I was so upset by my husband's uncaring attitude and unfaithfulness that after a couple of weeks, I went right back to eating again.

I craved peppermint candy and green apples for the entire nine months of pregnancy. And I couldn't sleep at night unless I had one or the other. I occasionally walked to the corner market and bought a few apples and a peppermint stick. But one day, I had neither in the house and no money.

When Louis came home from work, I asked him to get me apples or candy.

"You don't need apples and candy. You can go to sleep without them," he said.

But the craving was so strong, it was too difficult to sleep. I tossed and turned all night and only dozed occasionally.

When I first became pregnant, I weighed 95 pounds. But by the time I was ready to deliver, I had ballooned up to 145 pounds. I was much too heavy. I was in trouble, and I knew it.

Delivery day dawned early for me. The contractions had started the day before and had continued on and off throughout the night. I had sat up most of the night because the pain had kept me awake. I was so tired. Every time I dozed off, a contraction would hit with a jolt and wake me up.

I can't take this pain anymore, I thought to myself.

I decided to call the hospital at about eight o'clock in the morning.

"Has your water broken yet?" the nurse asked me.

"No, not yet," I replied. "but the contractions are so hard."

"Well, you're not ready if your water hasn't broken. Call me back when it does."

Louis was up getting dressed for work. I told him the baby was coming and he would have to take me to the hospital.

"I can't miss work," he said to me. "If you have to go, call a cab."

I stared at him in disbelief.

"But you have to take me," I said. "It's raining too hard. A cab will take forever to get here. And I'm afraid the baby is going to come soon."

"Well, I can't miss work."

I knew he could miss work if he wanted to. By the time he left, I was doubled over in pain and terribly frightened. How could I do this alone? My mind raced with what to do as I stared out our second-floor apartment window at the driving rain. I could barely see the creeping traffic below.

It had begun raining the day before, and we had had torrential rains for most of the night, and streets were flooded. I wanted to wait until it had stopped, but at that point, the contractions were so hard,

I had to grab on to a piece of furniture every time one hit. And the rain didn't look as if it was going to let up anytime soon.

I was afraid the baby would come while I was at home alone. I was a strong, healthy woman, but these last few days were proving to be a real challenge for me. I had heard of other women delivering their babies alone, but I wondered if they had been as frightened as I was or had as much pain as I was having right now. I had no idea I was going to be in this much pain.

Is it because I'm too heavy? I thought. *Well, it's too late now. I'll somehow just have to deal with* it.

The last thing I wanted to do was call a cab to take me to the hospital. Louis didn't even bother looking in the phone book to try and find one for me. He just pecked me on the cheek and left.

But the contractions kept getting closer together. And so by nine o'clock, I relented. When the cab arrived and the driver honked his horn, l lumbered down the stairs from our second-floor apartment, holding my stomach and an overnight bag.

Staring at the driver in dismay, I didn't want to go any further. He was a big, burly guy with a stomach that was almost as big as mine; and his shirt was unbuttoned right near his belly button, exposing it. His clothes looked as if he had slept in them, his cab was filthy, and he was smoking a fat cigar.

"Oh, we're gonna have a baby," he exclaimed jovially. "Are we going to the hospital?"

"Yes we are," I said, with an urgency in my voice.

"I've never delivered a baby before. Think I'd like to try it. Maybe I'll get to deliver this one."

Not if I can help it, I thought.

The rain was still coming down, and traffic was barely moving. Streets resembled giant parking lots. Visibility was no more than a few feet in front of us. That, coupled with the tortoise-like driving of the cabbie and his hopes of delivering his first baby made me more than a little bit nervous.

After what seemed like forever, we pulled into the army base and up to the curb of a building I didn't recognize. I had seen these buildings every day but had only been in the one where the clinic was. The cab driver lost interest once we arrived at the gate and the baby had not come. So he made it clear he had no intentions of driving me around to help me find where I was supposed to go.

I had barely gotten out and shut the door when, with tires squealing and showers of water spraying in all directions and drenching me as I exited, he sped away from the curb and disappeared without a word.

I didn't have time to be angry. As straight as I could, with suitcase in hand, I hurried into the building where he dropped me off and was told I was in the wrong place for delivery. There were so many buildings on the base, and except for the numbers on the front of them, they all looked the same. And the numbers were impossible to see in the rain.

I headed to the one place I had gone for my checkups during my pregnancy but was sent yet someplace else. The way this place was situated, it was difficult to follow the directions that were given to me.

Making my way through puddles and trying to see through the blinding rain, I reached the next building I had been sent to.

"No, they gave you the wrong one," I was told yet again. "You want the third building down across the street. Looks like you'd better hurry too."

The nurse had a concerned look on her face, but nobody in the office offered to help me, even though there were several staff workers there.

By then, I was shivering from the cold and soaked to the skin. My umbrella had long since become useless against the storm. So I folded it up, trying to concentrate on walking without slipping and falling down. I wasn't sure if I could make it to the right place in time, if indeed the person at the last desk had given me the correct information. It was a miracle I had gotten that far.

I trudged along as fast as I could, weakening with each step. A contraction hit so hard, I cried out in pain and reached out to grab hold of a telephone pole that I was passing by. I stood there, trying to hold on to the slippery pole to keep from falling until the stabbing pain passed.

People hurrying by with their heads bowed against the storm peered curiously from under their umbrellas at me. But my face could no longer hide the pain. I wept against the pole, praying that someone would stop and help me. No one did. I was afraid I was going to give birth on the sidewalk.

Please, God, help me, I prayed.

I made it to the next building I had been sent to. Thankfully, this time, I was in the right place. I didn't think I could take another step anyway. I was about to just sit down on the sidewalk in the cold rain.

In spite of my ordeal in the rain, labor was still long and hard, just like the doctor had said it would be, lasting nearly eighteen hours at the hospital alone. I didn't deliver until very late that night.

I was expecting Louis to stop by to see me after he got off work. But when he didn't show, I remembered this was his poker night and that's probably where he was. Nothing interfered with poker night. I didn't remember whose house the game was at this week, and neither could I remember any of his friends' phone numbers.

Did he even think about me all day? Does he know whether or not I was okay? I could only wonder.

The nurse kept calling our house but was unable to get a hold of him to tell him he had a son. She seemed surprised that he hadn't shown up and kept asking me where he was. I made the excuse he was probably working late. It wasn't until the next day she got a hold of him and he came by to see me. She looked at him rather sternly with a question in her eyes.

By the time my son was two years old, I realized that with all my efforts at trying to make it work, my marriage was over. How could I have gotten myself into this mess in the first place? How could I have been so naive?

I had tried very hard to be a good wife and mother, but Louis was self-centered and inconsiderate to me and even to his own children. I had developed a close relationship with them, but he was never there for them or me.

When the poker game was at our house, I made dessert and coffee as I usually did. They'd all sit around a card table in the living room, usually four or five couples, all friends of his. My place was on the couch behind them because I didn't know how to play poker. I felt awkward and unneeded sitting there, but Louis wanted me to stay there in case somebody needed more coffee or dessert. They played hard, cursed hard, laughed loud, and totally ignored me.

One night I decided I had had enough of playing maid to them, so unnoticed, I quietly slipped out and went to get ready for bed. About fifteen minutes later, Louis came into the bedroom looking for me.

"What are you doing back here?" he said. "We need more coffee."

"I'm getting ready for bed," I said to him nonchalantly.

"What do you mean you're getting ready for bed? You can't go to bed and just leave my friends out there. You're being rude to them."

I flashed him an angry look. "Your friends don't even acknowledge my presence unless they need something to eat or drink. I'm tired of sitting out there playing nursemaid to them."

A cold rage slowly formed in his eyes that made me freeze where I was standing. I braced myself, fearing he would hit me. I was afraid to keep standing there, and I was afraid to move.

With his jaw set, he hissed at me, "If you ever embarrass me like this again, I'll kill you."

He turned and went back to his game. I leaned on the dresser and closed my eyes. My heart was racing. Should I have just sat out there and continued to wait on them hand and foot? No. I was tired of all of them. Besides, I couldn't rectify things now. He's already mad.

I nervously dressed for bed and lay there, listening for his friends to leave. When I heard the door slam, my heart raced again. But after a while, when he hadn't come into the bedroom, I got up and tiptoed quietly through the house to see where he was. But he had left either with his friends or right behind them.

Relieved, I went back to bed but couldn't sleep. After glancing at the clock several times, I finally drifted off. I was awakened by the sound of the bedroom door opening and noticed it was 4:00 a.m. I pretended to be asleep as Louis quietly got in bed. At 6:00 a.m., he got up, dressed, and left the house without saying a word to me.

That morning, I mentally began to plan my escape, how I would get out of the house without him knowing I had permanently left and where I would go. I had never been so frightened of him before. And now I couldn't sleep at night because I was afraid he would carry out his threat to kill me. I had long been convinced I was only a convenience to have around to take care of his children. And now I knew his friends were more important to him than I was.

Days later when I had gathered more nerve to leave, I called my brother Bob in Los Angeles to find out that, if I needed a place to stay for a while, I could stay with him and his family. When he said I could, I then called Louis's best friend Bennie who was also one of his card playing buddies.

Bennie was always a gentleman, friendly, and courteous when he came to our house. He was the one friend of Louis's I knew I could trust. I confided to him that I was leaving Louis and asked him if he would take me and my son to the bus station, and he agreed.

"I told Louis this was gonna happen if he didn't start treating you better."

Bennie had told Louis many times that I was a good woman and he'd better start treating me better or he would come home one day and I would be gone. Louis told him he wasn't afraid of me leaving him because nobody else wanted me.

When I told Bennie what happened the night of the poker game, he was upset about it and apologized to me because he was there that night.

"I didn't know Louis said those awful things to you," he said. "We could have gotten our own coffee. It was no big deal."

He didn't realize that I sat there because Louis wanted me to.

Louis usually came home at odd hours, so I was a nervous wreck as I packed a few things to leave, freezing at every sound I heard. I hated leaving all our belongings behind, but I had no choice. I only packed one small suitcase with diapers and a change of clothes for the baby. I couldn't risk him walking in and catching me packing. Who knew what he might do?

I jumped as Bennie rang the doorbell. After leaving Louis a note on the bed explaining that I was leaving him because of the way he treated me and his kids, I locked the bedroom door and hurried out before he got home. I felt sorry for his sons, but there was no way I could take them with me.

Bennie quickly piled us and our meager luggage into his car and drove us to the Greyhound bus station, paid our fare, and gave me ten dollars for food and milk for Louie. I was so grateful for his help and asked Bennie to not tell Louis that he had helped me. He assured me he wouldn't because he didn't want to lose Louis's friendship.

Bennie hugged us, wished me good luck, and left us there. I was too nervous to sit down, so I held Louie in my arms and our bag in my hand and walked around in a panic, looking through the crowds, expecting Louie would find me before the bus showed up.

If only the bus would come, I hoped. *Please God, let the bus come. There are so many people waiting for busses, he could slip upon me before I could even see him.*

Momentarily, I'm reminded of the bus trip I took to Flint years a few years back where I had this same kind of fear. How could it be happening again?

Finally, our bus pulled up and then took forever to load us in and pull out. I was exhausted by the time we found a seat. After about an hour's ride, Louie fell asleep in my lap, and I was able to lay my head back on the seat and thank God for safe passage out of a bad marriage.

18

Is This the End?

I knew as soon as Louis got home and read my note, he would know I was gone for good. And he would soon figure out where I was. I found out later that he had called Daddy pretending to be Richard, just so Daddy would give him Bob's number. Daddy even said, "You sound funny."

"I have a bad cold. I lost Bob's number. Can you give it to me?"

When Daddy found out he had been tricked, he was furious, saying, "if I ever see him, I'll kill him."

After a few weeks at Bob's house, Louis began calling, begging me to come back home. I steadfastly refused to go back. One morning Bob and I had come back from dropping our children off at the babysitter's so we could both go to work, and Louis drove up behind us as Bob was parking the car. I had no idea he was even in Los Angeles.

He pretended to want to talk to me, but when Bob went in the house, leaving us outside, Louis grabbed my arm and tried to force me into his car. Screaming hysterically, I fought hard and wrestled away from him and ran up the stairs to my brother's apartment as fast as I could, losing my shoes on the way. Louis had put one hand into his pocket, and I could almost feel myself being shot in the back.

As I screamed Bob's name and pounded on the door, his wife Thelma yelled through the window and told me to keep my arguments outside. But I kept pounding and yelling until finally they opened the door slightly. I ran in and slammed the door behind me. Too scared to move away from the door, I thought he was going to shoot right through it.

Bob called the police, but Louis took off long before they arrived. The ordeal was very frightening, but the police said they couldn't do anything unless he hurt me. And I couldn't tell them where he came from or where he had gone. He didn't call me anymore after that.

A week later, I moved into my own apartment. I didn't hear anymore from him. Almost a year later, I received divorce papers in the mail. I was just beginning to relax and had thought he was going to leave me alone.

The papers showed a date had been set for a hearing. So that is how he was going to get back at me, I thought.

At the hearing, the judge gave Louis all the furniture and belongings in the house. He granted me custody of our son and gave Louis visitation rights. I told the judge in open court that I was afraid of my husband and that I didn't want him to know where I lived. I even told him about the gun incident. The judge matter-of-factly informed me that our marital problems were separate from visitation rights and that Louis still had a right to see his son.

On his first Friday visitation day, Louis arrived unannounced at my apartment at six o'clock in the evening. When I opened the door, he walked past me through the apartment without saying a word to me or my son and looked all around, even in the bathroom.

"What the heck are you doing?" I said.

"I just wanted to see who you had in here," he said as he came out and started inspecting all the cologne and hair items on the dresser. "Have you got a boyfriend?"

"That's none of your business," I told him.

"It is my business," he said.

Then in a flash, he turned, grabbed me, and, before I could react, began choking me.

"Mommy, Mommy!" my son started screaming.

"Get up in that chair and sit down and shut up," Louis yelled at him.

Terrified, Louie jumped up in the chair and immediately froze. I screamed and fought as hard as I could, but when he tightened his grip on my throat, I could no longer scream. He choked me until everything went black. When I awoke, I felt myself being carried from the couch to the bed. He laid me on the bed and then went over to the dresser and began removing my son's clothes out of the drawer.

"I'm taking my son with me," he said.

And then as if abruptly changing his mind, he left the drawer open and walked around to the side of the bed where I lay struggling to breathe, stepped back, and pulled out a small handgun.

He pointed it at my head and said in an even tone, "If I can't have you, nobody can."

Staring at the gun in his hand, I knew at that moment that my short life was over. I was going to die. I felt my head explode as he pulled the trigger once, twice, three times—the bullets violently striking me in the mouth, neck, and the back of the head, causing me to fall off the bed onto the floor. I fell in such a way that I could see his feet as he stood over me. He stood there for a few seconds, watching me. When I didn't move, probably figuring I was dead, he then hurried past me and my son out the front door.

What is going to happen to my baby? I thought when I couldn't see my son, lying in the position I was in.

As a pool of blood began to form around my head and widen out onto the carpet, I suspected the landlord would be angry at having his carpet ruined.

My upstairs neighbor had earlier knocked on the door when I was being choked and heard me screaming. Then when she heard the shots, she ran back up to her apartment and called the police. Moments later, they arrived, followed by the mournful wail of the ambulance siren.

Eight to ten policemen threw open the door and rushed in with guns drawn, crouching and then walking quickly past me through the small apartment, searching the bathroom, closets, and under the bed for anyone who might still be hiding there. The paramedics were not allowed to touch me until the house was cleared. Even the back alley was searched.

When they were satisfied no one else was in the apartment, one of them ordered, "Take that baby out of here."

By this time, my upstairs neighbor was standing on the porch, and she took Louie up to her apartment and tended to him that night, in spite of the fact that she had her own six children to care for.

One of the policemen leaned down close to me, felt my pulse and said, "She's still alive."

Noticing that I was still conscious, they pulled out pads and pens and began shooting questions at me, writing furiously.

"Who shot you? Where did he go? Where does he live? What is his phone number? His address? Did he have an accomplice?"

Still, the paramedics had not been given the okay to assist me.

It was not easy answering their rapid, sharp, pointed questions and trying to remember addresses and phone numbers while lying on the floor in a pool of blood.

Finally, the paramedics were given the go-ahead to treat me. And although in great pain, I remained conscious throughout the ambulance ride to the hospital.

"You're going to be all right," the attendant kept reassuring me, holding my hand tightly. "You're going to be all right."

But every now and then, he would glance quickly up front at the driver and, with an edge to his voice, say "Critical."

Each time he said it, we seemed to speed faster through traffic as the driver repeatedly honked his horn.

How ironic, I thought. As fast as we're going, I'm more likely to die from us crashing into another car than from these bullet wounds. I also noticed that the earsplitting siren was as loud inside as it was outside.

The hospital staff was bustling about amid all the activity of patients waiting to be seen by doctors, nurses calling for doctors over the intercom, and doctors rushing about.

They put me in a small room that looked more like a storage room than a hospital room. I laid there freezing for about ten minutes. Then a nurse came in and told me that the doctor was out playing golf and would not be back to do my surgery until Monday morning.

What an inappropriate remark to make to a person. She must be kidding.

"Hospitals have lots of doctors," I said.

And she replied curtly, "Well, your doctor won't be here until Monday."

"Who told you that? Nobody has even checked me yet."

She ignored my comment.

"I'm freezing. Can you put something over me?"

The nurse went out of the room and came back with a blanket, which she put on me, and then laid some kind of a form on top of the blanket and left the room. When she walked out of the room, the form fell on the floor. Of course I couldn't get up to get it.

She came back in a few minutes later and said to me, "Why did you throw that paper on the floor?"

"I didn't," I said. "It fell off the blanket on the floor."

"I don't believe you," she said.

But I was in too much pain to care. I just hoped the other nurses were in better moods than she was. After muttering and busying herself about for a few more minutes, she wheeled me out into a ward where I was transferred to a hospital bed.

Was it a coincidence that all the women on this ward had either attempted suicide or were victims of attempted homicides? I wasn't able to do much talking, but in listening to them, I learned that one's husband had tried to kill her.

Another young woman had attempted suicide by drinking a partial can of Drano. Her throat was permanently damaged so that she could only speak in a whisper. I wondered what had gone wrong in her life to bring her to this place. Her husband was there to visit her. Was he to blame? Had she experienced a bad marriage or had she been just so lonely she no longer wanted to live? I lay there wondering.

Another young woman sat on the side of her bed and stared vacantly into space, not talking to anyone.

At 9:00 p.m., I still had not been seen by a doctor since I arrived two hours earlier. I thought they were leaving me there to die. The searing pain in my head kept me from being able to close my eyes or sleep.

In desperation, I rang for a nurse. When she came in, I asked why nobody had been to check me since I had been admitted. She apologized and assured me that a doctor would be in shortly. She told me that it was a busy night and that they were short-staffed.

Shortly after she left, a doctor did come in to look at me.

"I'm sorry I couldn't see you earlier, but it's Friday night and we're really busy," the doctor said.

After a cursory look at my head, he asked me what happened. I briefly related the events of the evening.

"You are one lucky lady," he said, writing something on a chart and shaking his head. "I'm going to set you up for surgery on Monday. And don't worry. You're going to be okay."

"Is it true that the doctor who's going to do my surgery is playing golf?" I asked.

"Who told you that?"

"The rude nurse in the admitting section."

I could tell he was displeased.

"She shouldn't have told you that. But you'll be in good hands. Dr. Gray is a fine doctor."

"But the pain is so bad, I don't know if I can make it until Monday."

"I'll give you something for the pain. I'm going to start an IV on you, and you'll start feeling better soon. And I'll give you something to help you sleep too."

The medication caused the pain in my head to ease slightly, but it didn't go away.

What would happen to Louie if I died? Who would take care of him? I couldn't bear the thought of my stepmother getting her hands on him. I knew she'd probably beat him as she had beaten me. But I was, at the moment, helpless. I didn't have any say-so over anything. I wanted so much to see my son grow up. But what could I do?

Monday morning finally came. I had had a lonely, scary weekend and also a fear that I might, at any moment, open my eyes to find Louis standing over me.

A bright and chipper attendant came in early and told me, "We're going to do surgery on you this morning, and then you'll feel much better."

"Are you sure?"

"Yes, I'm sure," he smiled. "The doctors here are very good."

Humming to himself, he and another staff person gently placed me on a gurney and wheeled me down a bleak, sterilized long hallway.

I tried to look back, hoping to see some familiar face. But there was not one soul. As they wheeled me into the room, I tried to get one last longing gaze, wanting desperately for someone to be with me, to hold my hand. No one.

I may not come out of this room alive. Somebody, anybody, I screamed inside my head.

The massive room they wheeled me into was icy cold and full of machinery. They transferred me from the gurney on to a table and tied my hands to the table. I became frightened at being restrained. And with nothing on except a light hospital gown, I began to shiver. This time, there was no blanket.

Then they left me, went out, and closed the door. Lying there cold, I scanned the room. The large, gold-and-white clock up on the wall off to my right side stared back at me in slow motion. What a stark reminder of aloneness, I thought.

I wondered how long I was going to lie there.

I'm so cold. I wish they had put something over me, I said to myself. *And why did they have to tie my hands? Did they think I was going to try and run away? Where would I go?*

I could hear occasional voices in the hallway, but no one came into the room. And I could not call out, for no one could hear me anyway. I had only the clock for company.

After staring at it for forty-five long minutes, the door opened, and a team of doctors in surgical scrubs entered the room.

"Good morning, Gloria," one said from behind his mask. "How are you feeling?"

"I'm cold."

"We'll take care of that. I want you to start counting backward from one hundred for me.

"One hundred, ninety-nine, ninety-eight..."

I awoke two days later to discover that I was still alive and that I had been in surgery for nine hours. I couldn't turn my head, and I couldn't talk. And when I tried to speak, no words came out. The pain was, at times, unbearable. I tried to remember what had happened and why I couldn't talk, but my brain was fuzzy.

Later in the day, when my head began to clear, my doctor stopped by. I became quite distressed to find out from him that the bullets had not been removed. I thought that was what the surgery was for.

"It was too dangerous to try and remove them," he insisted." You would have died on the table. We were more concerned about saving your life, so we decided to leave them in. They will have to come out later, if at all."

I remained on the critical list for seven days and was in the hospital for nearly three weeks. A few days after surgery, when I was able to get out of bed, I walked somewhat unsteadily to the bathroom to look at my face and was shocked at the image that stared back at me.

With my head completely bandaged and my face partially bandaged, I very much resembled a war casualty. The right side of my face was paralyzed and had the appearance of melted wax from my eye down to my chin. My ability to speak had been severely hampered, and my right eye would not close.

When they brought me food, I found I couldn't open my mouth wide enough to get a spoon in. With patience and manipulation, I could open it just enough to slide a fork partially in. Swallowing was very difficult. And when I tried to put the fork in my mouth, the food would fall back on to the tray.

The only soft food they brought was mashed potatoes at dinnertime, which became the only food I was able to swallow because my facial muscles no longer worked and I couldn't chew anything. So all the food, except the potatoes, went back to the kitchen on the tray. I was very frustrated because I was still hungry.

I tried to tell the nurses I couldn't eat the food they were bringing, but they couldn't understand what I was saying. When they brought me steak, all I could do was stare at it. Making motions to the nurses trying to make them understand I couldn't eat the food didn't help. The menu didn't change.

Different doctors came daily to change my bandages. There wasn't much communication with them because they couldn't understand me either. They would talk to me, but I couldn't talk back. I made gestures to them or, if I could find paper, I wrote notes. I wrote that the pain was constant and I couldn't sleep.

One of the doctors promised to give me something stronger, although nothing they gave me helped very much, so I stopped complaining. I also asked each one who came in when if I would be able to talk and turn my head again. Each one, in turn, avoided my eyes as they all said, "Pretty soon."

When Dr. Gray came days later to take the stitches out, he noticed my anxiety and smiled at me.

"I'm nervous," I said.

"Don't worry, it won't hurt," he said. "You've been through the worst part already."

He pulled up a chair and sat close to the bed as he carefully worked to slowly remove the stitches one by one. He was very patient, and he talked to me the whole time, trying to keep me distracted as much as possible.

It took a long time, but he was partially right. The stitches behind my ear did hurt, but the ones that ran down the side of my scalp were just uncomfortable. I was very tense, which probably added to the discomfort.

Gently taking the stitches out one by one, Dr. Gray said, "I did a pretty good job for my first surgery, if I do say so myself."

"You're kidding," I said, trying to keep my head still. "I was your first surgery?"

"Yes, my first major surgery," he added proudly. "You know, we thought you were going to die. We didn't hold out much hope for you at all. But you came through. You're very lucky to be alive."

"I didn't think I was going to make it either. By the way, Doctor, how many stitches do I have?

"Ninety-nine."

"Why didn't you make it an even hundred?" I jokingly said to him.

He threw his head back and laughed.

"You know, I didn't think about it."

He seemed to be the only one who could understand me.

Finally ready to leave the hospital, I was a sight to see. Still bandaged and looking more like I was on my way home from Vietnam, I at least was alive. Now I had to decide where to go. Afraid to return to my apartment, my boyfriend Harry's mother invited me to stay with her until I could find another place to live.

While there, Mother Beamon, a wonderful Christian lady who was a friend of Harry's family, was taking care of my son. When she heard I was out of the hospital, she brought him by to see me. I was so bandaged and swollen, Louie shied away from me at first because he didn't recognize me. I'm sure I must have frightened him.

But even though I couldn't talk very well, after talking to him a little bit, he began to recognize my voice and come closer. He then climbed up in my lap and stared at my face. He lifted his little hand and began to pat my bandages and hold me tight.

And when Mother Beamon tried to take him, he held on tighter and wouldn't leave me. I told her it would be okay to leave him since I was feeling a little better. So he ended up staying with me the remaining time I was there, staring a lot at my face, rarely leaving my side.

I stayed with Harry's family for a month until I was able to find another apartment. Still not able to turn my head, I couldn't drive. So I took the bus back and forth to the doctor, which was about the only place I dared go, considering how I looked and the stares I got from people.

Three months after I left the hospital, Louis was finally caught and arrested. I testified against him at his preliminary hearing, explaining exactly how the shooting happened.

But his attorney unsuccessfully argued to the judge that the gun was mine and I had pulled it on him. We struggled over it, and it went off three times, shooting me. He said that it was just a domestic dispute. He didn't allow Louis to testify.

I was shocked at the blatant lies Louis had told his attorney. And how could this attorney be so callous as to say those terrible things? He could see I still bore terrible scars, and the swelling in my face still hadn't gone down yet. The judge didn't believe their side and bound Louis over for trial.

The day before I was to appear in court to testify against him, I decided to call the courthouse to be sure of the time I was supposed to show up for my testimony.

When I got the clerk on the line, he said to me, "His case has been dismissed."

"What?" I said. "That's impossible. His trial starts tomorrow. He's still in jail."

"He was released yesterday."

"He couldn't have been released. Why was he released? He tried to kill me. This can't be."

"Lady, I've got other things to do and other cases to handle. I don't know why he was released other than the district attorney's office failed to bring him to trial within the sixty-day time limit, so the judge dismissed his case. If we don't bring him to trial in sixty days, his case has to be dismissed. That's the law, and that's all I know."

My head was reeling, and my stomach was nauseous when I hung up the phone.

How could this be happening?

I sat at my desk with my head in my hands. It was only a few minutes after nine, and I knew my boss wouldn't let me go home. But there was no way I would be able to concentrate on my work for eight hours. I didn't want to be around people anymore. I just wanted to go in a corner and cover my face.

When I walked into my boss's office, he could tell something was wrong.

"What happened?" he said. "what's the matter?"

Struggling to hold back the tears, I explained the phone call.

"I can't believe it," he said. "Were they not even going to tell you?"

"I guess not. I would have showed up at court tomorrow for nothing. I know I just got here, but I can't work today. Can I please have the day off?"

"Oh, Gloria, I'm sorry. I wish I could give you the day off, but I need you. We've got a ton of orders to fill. And I need everybody until we can get our heads above water."

As upset as I was, I knew he was right. We supplied saline solution and drugs to hospitals and had been bombarded with a rush of orders for the past week due to the recent addition of four more hospitals to our list of customers. I was my boss's personal secretary, plus I operated a computer filling orders. It was a long and painful day.

My doctor had explained to me upon leaving the hospital that the paralysis to the right side of my face was permanent. My ability to talk had been severely diminished, and my right eye still would not close.

Even though he said he didn't think it would help, he made an appointment for me to begin undergoing speech therapy to learn how to talk again. So despite my workload, for a while, I was having to leave work early to go for treatments three times a week.

The first day I showed up for speech therapy, I inquired at the information desk where the speech therapy clinic was, but nobody could understand a word I said. Eventually, it resembled a game of charades as all the patients in the waiting room chimed in to try and help the staff understand what I was trying to say. I was getting embarrassed by the attention.

Finally, one of the staff said, "Oh, I know what you want. You're looking for speech therapy."

"Right." I nodded my head, relieved.

Then walking down the hall past the emergency room, several patients were sitting in the hallway in chairs waiting to be seen by doctors. As I passed them, every one of them stared at me. One older gentleman shook his head and whispered to his companion sitting next to him, "Poor thing."

The speech therapist had to test me first to find out how much of my nerve function was lost. She talked cheerfully and assured me that it was going to be a painless test.

After having me lie on the table and hooking me to what seemed like hundreds of tubes, she turned on the electricity.

The shock to my head, face, and upper body was so severe, I screamed and jumped completely off the table. Tubes went flying, and the nurse almost did too. She was so nervous and apologetic, she had to sit down for a few minutes to regain her composure.

"I am so sorry. I am so, so sorry," she kept saying. "I had no idea that was going to happen. I didn't mean to hurt you. Do you want to try it again today or you want to come back?"

"Oh, no. I want to do it now, just a little milder, please."

"Oh, don't worry. I won't do that again."

She hooked me up again, her hands still slightly shaking. Even when she said "you can relax for sure this time," I was still completely tensed up. I could feel the shock run down the side of my face, but this time it was so mild, it was almost imperceptible.

"Now we want to try and stimulate the nerves in your face to work again," she said, "so we give them what we call shock treatments—mild at first and then a little more intense. But I promise you it will never be like the first one."

She turned the electricity on and off, from mild to intense, for about fifteen minutes. I could feel the electricity go through my head and neck, but it was bearable. Then she had me try other things like blowing up a balloon, an impossible task which I never mastered. When she gave me a glass of water to drink, the water poured down the front of my clothes. Then she had me attempt to turn my head in either direction, which I couldn't do even a little bit. I was still forced to turn my whole body.

Each time I went for therapy, besides the electric shock, she tried various things, none of which ever worked.

I underwent these electric shock treatments for three months. And then at my next regular appointment, my doctor told me, "You can stop going for the shock treatments. According to the therapists and the test results, they are not helping at all, and there is nothing more they can do for you."

He handed me a little black box that looked like a child's ABC block.

"This is a little electric shock box that will do mild treatments at home."

He showed me how to use it. It registered so mildly that I knew it wouldn't work for me if the big one in the hospital didn't. But I was willing to try it anyway.

Up to now, the nerves in my face were still unresponsive to treatment, my face was still horribly distorted, and I was still having severe headaches.

I continued to have outpatient doctor visits. As the months went on, limited speech returned; but the paralysis remained, and my face was severely twisted. When I tried to move my mouth and my eye, nothing happened. My whole face felt and looked like a piece of stone. I couldn't move anything on the right side. My skin began to appear dry and ashen.

I'd look in the mirror and think to myself, *This is what you must look like when you die.*

My hair had been shaved completely off the right side of my head from the center straight back. My scalp had a fine film of what looked to be dandruff that was visible on close inspection and crept down into my face.

When I went out in public, I wore a scarf, no matter what the weather because of my baldness and the wind. Even though my face was paralyzed, I could still feel pain, and even the slightest breeze on the right side was excruciating. So I shielded my face with the scarf and turned my head away from the wind to avoid the onslaught of a massive headache.

My head was too sore and tender to wear a wig. And I couldn't wash the ashen look from my face because the slightest touch caused excruciating pain. I couldn't touch my cheeks with my fingers, let alone a washcloth.

People stared as they passed me on the street. Some even let their curiosity get the best of them as they would come right up to me and ask me, "What happened to your face?"

I would say "I got shot" as politely as I could but also try to ward off further conversation about the incident.

One man stared and stared at me while I was sitting in court at one of my divorce hearings, making me uncomfortable. He finally walked over and asked me, "Did you have a tooth pulled today?" Even in church, I heard my name whispered.

One Sunday morning, I looked across the lobby to see two women with their heads together discussing me. When they saw me look at them, they stopped talking.

After several months of outpatient visits, I was sitting in my doctor's office one day, avoiding the stares that I had become so accustomed to. All at once, my face twitched, ever so slightly. It was almost imperceptible but real, nonetheless.

In shock, I gripped the arms of the chair I was sitting in. My eyes widened. No one could tell from my expression that anything had happened. But inside, I was overjoyed and couldn't wait to tell the doctor.

When the nurse called me in, I almost ran past her. Since I was so difficult to understand, I tried to remain calm as I excitedly said, "Doctor, my face moved!"

"What?" the doctor said, not thinking he heard me right.

"My face moved," I mouthed excitedly, pointing to the area where I had felt the twitch.

I was so happy, I tried to smile, but my face still showed no emotion.

"No it didn't," he said matter-of-factly.

"Yes it did. I felt it. It was a slight twitch, but I felt it."

He sat me down and pulled up his stool directly in front of me. He took both of my hands in his. There was compassion in his eyes, and he looked as if he wanted to cry. I almost felt sorry for him.

He looked me straight in the face and with a tremor in his voice said very seriously, "Gloria, the paralysis to your face is permanent. You are going to have to accept that. The bullets that were used shattered on impact, causing extensive, irreversible damage. There are numerous fragments, and they are still imbedded in your face, your neck, and your skull because we couldn't remove them without killing you. Major nerves were destroyed. The nerves that control movement of the face were destroyed. You will never talk normally again, you will never turn your head again, and you will never move your face again."

Since the accident, I had not yet been able to turn my head from side to side. It would not move in any direction, and constantly turning my whole body was very tiring.

But at that moment, something rose up on the inside of me. I returned the doctor's stare and with slurred speech and a twisted grimace that I meant to be a smile, I said, "Oh yes I will."

Try as I might, though, months passed before I felt the next twitch. But it came, and then months later, the next one, and the next one. Each time, I gained a little more confidence.

Slowly my speech improved to where I didn't have to write things down to make myself understood. Even the doctor was beginning to take notice. He was pleased and surprised. The swelling in my face went down, which took away some of the distortion. My hair had begun to grow back.

I learned that if I talked slowly and without smiling, I could be understood. The paralysis slightly diminished. I decided if God had been gracious enough to let me live, then I would do all I could to live my life as fully as I could.

I was still working hard at my job, but the pay was low, and I was struggling to raise my son. I learned to be creative in cooking and keeping our tiny apartment on my small salary.

Eventually, I knew if I ever wanted better employment, I would have to go to school. After explaining to Mother Beamon my desires to attend court reporting school, she readily agreed to babysit for me in the evenings.

Mother Beamon babysat all the children in the neighborhood. There were so many kids in her house on the weekends, it was hard to tell who was being babysat and who was just visiting. The mothers all trusted her, and the children all loved her. As a young mother, she even taught me things I probably should have learned at home but didn't.

She had an unmistakable strength about her and a kindness I had not seen in many people. I could confide in her without feeling stupid, and I knew her advice would be sound. She treated me like a daughter and my son like her own.

Even after some of our children outgrew the need for a babysitter, they would still call each other up and arrange to spend the weekends at her house. She always had a houseful of teenagers on the weekends.

She refused to accept money from me for babysitting Louie. She'd say matter-of-factly, "You can't afford it. You and that baby need to eat."

I couldn't figure out how she knew I had no money because I never told her. But she was right. I was really struggling.

But since she wouldn't accept my money, even though she protested, I bought her groceries every week and special things I knew she liked. She loved lamb chops but couldn't afford to buy them on her meager pension. So I bought them for her, along with eggs and flour so she could make her delicious cookies, or "tea cakes," as she called them.

I knew babysitters were expensive, so I considered myself really lucky to have her. She was such a dear lady, and I couldn't let her just keep Louie for free.

She made tea cakes almost daily for all the kids whom she babysat and also for her church, where she sold them for a quarter a bag. Each bag contained four to six big, fat cookies. Louie and I always got a bunch free to take home. She wouldn't hear of me paying her for them.

Getting through court reporting school was one of the hardest things I had ever done. Louie was young; and it hurt me to come home from work, pick him up from school, and take him directly to Mother Beamon's house. He missed me and wanted to go home.

And the nights that it rained or the nights he cried to go home always turned out to be the nights I had a test that I couldn't miss. Many nights, I cried all the way to school. Even though I knew he was happy with Mother Beamon and all the other kids that she had there, I felt like such a bad mother leaving him there to go to school four nights a week.

During my last year of school, I had been thinking about leaving my job, getting a part-time job, and going to both day school and night school so I would be sure to finish within the year. Not only was I plain tired of going to school at night, it was very stressful and grueling. I wanted to do all I could to make the fourth year my last year.

So I let all my vacation time at work accumulate until I had three weeks. My supervisor tried to tell me I couldn't take it all at once, but I knew he was trying to intimidate me into not using it all at the same time. The company just didn't want any employee to be gone that long. But legally, he knew he couldn't stop me. He was angry when I told him I needed to take it all.

What a vacation it turned out to be. It was just about the toughest three weeks ever. Every single day I was in class, plus four nights. But by the end of the three weeks, I had covered about six months' worth of classes. By then, I knew If I continued going to day school, I would be able to graduate by year's end. And so I decided that was the way to go.

I went in to my supervisor and explained the situation to him. I asked him to lay me off so that I could collect unemployment while looking for a part-time job and finish my schooling.

"I can't do that," he said to me. "I can't lay you off just so you can go to school."

"Then give me a leave of absence. Come on, Rick," I said. "I'm trying to better myself. You knew this day would come where I would eventually have to leave."

"I'm sorry, but you can't go. We need you, and I can't accommodate your request."

"Well then, I'll just have to quit."

"You can't quit. You have a son to raise."

"I'm aware of that. But I have to do this. I've been going to night school for three years, and it's time I put my all into this so that I can graduate this year."

When he saw I was serious and he couldn't deter me, he said, "I'll give you three months, and you'll come crawling back."

He was loud, angry, and abusive. Shocked at his sarcastic attitude, that statement alone was enough for me to walk out the door with my head held high, determined he would not be the one to dictate my life.

"I can promise you that no matter what happens, I won't come crawling back here," I said to him.

I put in my two weeks' notice. I had been a good employee and had a good relationship with everybody at the company, bosses included. I didn't want to leave on a bad note, even though I knew Rick was just mad because he was losing a good employee.

Inquiring around school, I discovered there was an opening for a part-time secretarial position not far from my school at the Hall of Administration. And after going in for an interview, I was hired. The pay wasn't very high for four hours a day, but it allowed me to go to school in the mornings and work there in the afternoons.

After graduating that same year from reporting school, I obtained a job with a deposition agency and began doing depositions around town. I enjoyed the work, but the commute was hard, not only on me, but also my car, not knowing from day to day how far

I was going to have to travel. And many times I was short on money and low on gas.

What I really wanted to do was work in court and was eventually lucky enough to land a job with an agency who used reporters in court. They soon advised me of an opening in the Compton courthouse, and asked me if I were interested. It was exactly what I wanted. I loved it. The pay was more, my hours were steady, and I enjoyed working with the people.

But even though I was busy and my days and evenings were divided between my job and my son, I battled terrible loneliness. Being a single mom was hard, but having no family and no real friends around was just as hard. I felt like I had a hole in my heart.

After such a struggle to get where I was, I began to wake up in the mornings, dreading going to work. Where was the anticipation for a new day? Something was missing.

I would go home after work, and the walls seemed to close in on me. Occasionally I picked up the telephone just to make sure it was still working because it rarely rang.

Then I started thinking, *What's the use? Why have I come this far? Nobody cares.*

I began entertaining the thought of suicide. When I woke up in the morning, I thought about it. All during the day, I thought about it. When I went to bed at night, I thought about it. I wasn't worried about how I would do it. I surely wasn't going to make a mistake. I was just contemplating when.

My son was a little older now, but I felt I wasn't a good enough mother and he needed somebody better. But who would love him more than I did? I was going to have to really plan this thing.

Nobody knew him better than me and Mother Beamon. She would be the perfect person. But she was getting to be near seventy. I didn't know how long she would live. I wanted an out, but I couldn't find one.

I began praying for a change in my life. I didn't know how to pray eloquently, so I just talked to God as if He were a friend. I knew if I prayed earnestly enough, He would hear me. After all, He had heard me before.

19

I Want What She's Got

My days off were rare, but my neighbor Belia had a sixth sense when those days came. She would walk across the driveway that separated our apartments and knock on my door early in the morning. I wondered who it could be that early in the morning because nobody knew I was home. And there she stood smiling. We were good neighbors. Our children played together. Her sister Sally later moved next door to me in apartment C.

"How did you know I was home?" I'd say, smiling, glad for the company.

"I don't know. I just had a feeling."

We'd take off driving to Huntington Park to window-shop. We rarely had more than five dollars between us. We'd buy a soda and walk around, look in all the stores, and just enjoy each other's company. Once in a while, if we had money, we'd go have breakfast at Norm's. I don't know who had more fun than we did.

On one of those rare days, she rapped on my door with her usual quote, "I just had a feeling you were home." But one day, there was something different about her. I just couldn't pinpoint what it was.

"Guess what?" she said.

"What?"

"I got saved."

"That's great," I said, trying to sound enthusiastic. I didn't know what it felt like to be saved, even though I had always prayed for as long as I could remember.

She was so bubbly, her joy spilled over into my kitchen, making it brighter. We didn't go-window shopping that day. We spent our time together talking about her conversion. I found myself engrossed in her wonderful experience.

How I wish I could relate, I thought, as I watched her face simply radiate with the love of Jesus.

When she left my house, the sunshine left with her. I walked into my kitchen, which now seemed devoid of light. Even the sun had gone behind the clouds. Standing there staring into space, I longed for Jesus more than ever.

From the depths of my soul, I cried, "Lord, I want what she's got. If you really are who you say you are, come into my heart and change me."

I didn't feel any earthshaking change at all. But I thought about Belia constantly after that. Was it possible that I could ever be that joyful? That ecstatic? That full of life? The void inside me grew.

A week or so after that incident, their car broke down and had to be put in the shop for repairs. That Friday, Belia came over and told me that her nephew Victor's birthday party was that night and they had no way to get to it. And since the car wasn't ready, Belie asked if I would mind driving them to the party.

I didn't mind because it gave Louie and me something to do. He would enjoy playing with all the other kids.

Music was coming from the kids' bedroom when we got there. Victor and several of his friends were in his bedroom playing games and dancing. The adults were in the kitchen laughing and talking. Not listening intently, I picked up that they were talking about Jesus.

I sat at the kitchen table watching them but not taking part. They had the same glow on their faces as Belia had the day she told me she had gotten saved.

One of the women looked over at me and announced, "We're going to pray for Gloria before we go home."

"Oh, no, you're not," I said, suddenly taken aback by complete strangers wanting to pray for me.

They ignored my comment and continued talking. But I now concentrated on keeping my defenses up.

The only people I knew at the party was Belia, her sisters Sally and Jenny, and their children. The rest of the people there I had never seen before.

When the party finally ended, everyone began leaving to go home, I thought, *Oh, good, they forgot.*

And then somebody said, "Come on, Gloria. Sit right here."

Somebody put a chair in the middle of the living room, and I reluctantly sat on it. Now we had a living room full of adults, and all those who could reach me laid their hands on my head and my shoulders and began praying. I really felt foolish. Then all at once I started crying.

Wait a minute, I thought. *I'm losing control. This is not supposed to be happening.*

But I couldn't stop crying. And the more I cried, the cleaner I began to feel inside, as if the tears were washing all the dirt away. And the strangest thing of all happened—I began to feel happy.

And then they were all hugging me. They kept telling me, "You're saved. You're saved," although I wasn't quite sure what had just happened.

On the way home, I had Belia, her husband Joe, and all our kids in my car; and they were all laughing hysterically.

"Gloria, I'm not sure we should have let you drive. You're all but driving on the sidewalk. I hope we all get home safe."

"Do you know how long I've been praying for this?" I bubbled. "I've never felt joy like this in my whole life. Everybody should have this kind of joy."

I was so happy with my new life that I wanted to please the Lord in every way possible. I praised Him and thanked Him for caring enough to save me, for nobody had ever loved me before. I even noticed I no longer wanted to commit suicide.

One morning about a week later, the alarm went off in my ear at 5:30 a.m., which was time for me to get up for work. I lay there momentarily, trying to pry my eyes open so I could roll out onto the floor before I dozed back off. Moments later, I was up.

Making my way to the bathroom with sleep still clouding my eyes, a clear and distinct voice spoke to me, *"You have to forgive her."*

The voice was so clear and so loud, I turned around to see who was there. It came from everywhere and nowhere. But I was alone in the house, except for my son sleeping on the couch. I knew it was the Lord, and I knew exactly whom he was talking about.

I leaned weakly against the wall.

"Oh, Lord, I can't. I can't," I said. "There's too much pain. All those years of abuse and mistreatment. How can I forgive her for that? We didn't deserve what happened to us. We were in her way through no fault of our own."

"But you hated her and you still do," the Lord spoke to me again. *"You can't serve me with hatred in your heart."*

He got me there. I didn't have an argument for that one because it was absolutely true. The hatred I felt for my stepmother was cancerous. It had been eating away at me daily for years.

"But, Lord," I said, "isn't there some other way? Can't you just dissolve this bitterness and make me clean without me having to go to her?"

But heaven was silent. God had spoken, and there was nothing I could do but obey.

I had thought that by joining the army, I was getting away from my stepmother forever and that the bad feelings I had toward her would go away if I didn't have to be around her. That didn't work. I had served my time and come out, and I still hated her.

I had learned that I couldn't run away from my problems or my past. I would have to turn and face them sooner or later. And I had been able to do that with certain things, but not this.

I thought as time went on that all the bitterness was gone, but throughout the years, different incidents in my life would bring back childhood memories of the abuse I had suffered. The hatred that lay dormant in my heart would rise to the surface like some silent monster, anxious to attack.

I tried telling myself I had turned out to be a good citizen and a responsible adult so my past didn't matter. And besides, I was justified in having these feelings because I only noticed them once in a while. But I couldn't shake the guilt I felt.

So after God and I had this conversation, I decided to pray about it all week and then call home on Sunday. I didn't know what I would say. I would just have to depend on Him to help me.

The week passed swiftly, and Sunday came all too soon. I went to church, hoping He would speak to me again, giving me an alternate route to take. But no sound came from heaven. I sure didn't want to speak on the phone. My heart was so heavy; I didn't hear any part of the pastor's sermon that Sunday.

Detroit time was three hours ahead of us, so I knew Sunday would be the best day to call because my parents always went straight home after church. I waited as long as I could Sunday afternoon but finally decided to get it over with. I was hoping they weren't home. If they were not home, I wouldn't call back. At least I will have tried.

Wouldn't you know it? My stepmother answered the phone. I wasn't sure how to begin. We talked about the weather, world peace, and everything else in between that I could think of, all in five minutes.

"Mama, I just want to ask you to forgive me for anything I ever did to make your life miserable or to make you miss out on anything you ever wanted and didn't get while you were raising us," I finally said. "Forgive me for anything I have ever done to hurt you. I truly do apologize."

I said a few more things because I didn't want to leave anything out.

"Oh, you know I forgive you," she said.

We talked a little bit more, and I said I would keep in touch. When I hung up the phone, I felt as light as a feather. It was as if a huge boulder had fallen off my shoulders. I was sure Jesus and His angels were smiling down upon me like the sun smiles down upon a flower.

And just as a flower responds to sunshine by raising its petals heavenward, I raised my hands to God in thanksgiving. I felt free and loved. I was happier than I had ever been. Now I knew real joy. Why had it taken me so long to do this? For the first time in my life, I had absolutely no bitterness toward my stepmother. My heart was light and right.

SMALL SPACE

I was mildly surprised that she didn't ask me for forgiveness, but I decided that that was between her and God. I had done what I had to do.

I also began praying for my ex-husband and for the ability to forgive him. I knew I had to have God's help with the bitterness I had for him too.

Soon after my conversion, I got another rare day off. This time, I was expecting the knock at my door. Sure enough, peeking out through the peephole, there stood my smiling friend, Belia.

"Don't tell me. You just had a feeling," I said.

"You know I did," she said, laughing delightfully. "Don't ask me how I always know, but I do."

Feeling free, that day, I could laugh with her.

"Let's splurge today. Let's go to Huntington Park to window-shop and Norm's for breakfast. I got breakfast money."

"Oh, good."

We took off in my car, happily chattering all the way.

Once at Norm's, perusing the menu, Belia asked, "I don't know what I want. What are you going to have?"

Smiling wryly, I mused out loud, "Well, first, I think I'll have a bowl of oatmeal."

About the Author

Gloria Hall received her certified shorthand reporter (CSR) degree in 1978 from Bryan College of Court Reporting and has been a court reporter in Los Angeles County for twenty-two years.

Gloria has taught leadership training and has traveled with district leaders to Southeast Asia, touring and ministering in Singapore, Malaysia, Hong Kong, and Mainland China. She has written for the national church magazine, the *Evangel*.

Ms. Hall is active in her local church. She has been president of her women's ministries group for the past fourteen years. For many years, Gloria sang in her church choir. She presently is part of the praise team and is an accomplished soloist.

Despite all her suffering, God has given Gloria a compassionate heart, and she takes every opportunity to reach out to those in need. Gloria heads the homeless ministry More Than a Meal, where she prepares seventy-five to one hundred sack lunches and care packages containing socks, toiletries, bottled water, Bibles and tracks, clothes, shoes, and blankets, which she distributes every Saturday morning to those lining the streets and underpasses of skid row. She encourages and assures each one of God's love for them.

Indulging in her passion for cooking, Gloria has written a cookbook entitled *Favorite Homestyle Recipes*. Gloria has one son, Louis, who is an architect. Gloria is also a graduate of Florence Littauer's advanced CLASS (Christian Leaders and Speakers Seminars).

www.ingramcontent.com/pod-product-compliance
Lightning Source LLC
LaVergne TN
LVHW040100080526
838202LV00045B/3719